THE MENTALITY OF
SUCCESS

Copyright © 2022 by Joshua Washington

Published by Kudu Publishing

All rights reserved. No portion of this book may be reproduced, stored in a retrieval system, or transmitted in any form or by any means—electronic, mechanical, photocopy, recording, scanning, or other—except for brief quotations in critical reviews or articles, without prior written permission of the author.

For foreign and subsidiary rights, contact the author.

Cover design by Sara Young
Cover Photos by Tatianna Laboy and Joris Bruno

ISBN: 978-1-957369-07-5   1 2 3 4 5 6 7 8 9 10

Printed in the United States of America

THE MENTALITY OF SUCCESS

🔒 ACTIVATE YOUR DREAMS,
UNLOCK YOUR POTENTIAL

JOSHUA WASHINGTON

Dedication

*This book is dedicated to
my son—Nehemiah Lee Washington.
I pray that even when I'm long gone, you will still hear
Daddy cheering you on through these pages.
Remember: Success is your destiny!
Jeremiah 29:11*

CONTENTS

Introduction 9

CHAPTER 1. Dreams 21

CHAPTER 2. Discovery 63

CHAPTER 3. Development 107

CHAPTER 4. Decisions: The Land of Clarity 145

CHAPTER 5. Conclusion 165

Acknowledgments 171

About the Author 175

INTRODUCTION

YOUR MENTALITY

Picture an empty field. One that extends as far as your eyes can see. The grass is rich, healthy, and green, and the fresh smell of spring, which signals growth is on the horizon, is in the air. This field is an analogy of your brain right before the building begins. Soon, construction will start, and on this land, an occupied city will exist. The city I'm referring to represents your mentality. Picture it as a collection of large buildings occupying the land within your mind. The quality of these buildings represents the quality of your mentality.

A high-quality mentality consists of your outlook on four core mentalities. These core mindsets determine whether or not you experience a life of fulfillment. These four pillars are the Mentalities of Success, Leadership, Wealth, and Faith. Show me anyone who has developed healthy structures in these four areas, and I will show you someone that is experiencing great levels of purpose, hope, and fulfillment.

> **Show me anyone who has developed healthy structures in these four areas, and I will show you someone that is experiencing great levels of purpose, hope, and fulfillment.**

This book will only focus on one of the core four: *The Mentality of Success*. The roadmap to identifying purpose and defining success in your life requires that you journey through four zones:

- → Dreams.
- → Discovery.
- → Development.
- → Decisions.

As you see in the figure below, these zones are split into pairs. While the dreams and discovery zones focus more on assessment, the development and decisions zones are all about execution (gaining a return on your value). This is important to know as the first two zones will require that you ask some tough questions, assess areas of your life, and examine thoughts that you may not have considered before. Don't let that overwhelm you; the answers are already around you and within you. The second pair of zones focus on implementation and execution. Awareness is great; however, awareness that evolves into action and execution is the goal. The development and decisions portion of this book will provide you with a roadmap on how to execute gaining a return on your value and leaving a lasting legacy. Before we dive deeper into these concepts, though, it is important to first define *The Mentality of Success*.

A		E	
DREAMS	**DISCOVERY**	**DEVELOPMENT**	**DECISIONS**
SEARCH OF DESTINY	UNPACKING YOU	GAINING A RETURN	BUILDING A LEGACY

THE MENTALITY OF SUCCESS

What does success mean to you? How do you measure it? When you close your eyes and picture yourself as a "success," what do you see? Take a moment and think about these questions. No, really, put down this book, grab a blank sheet of paper, draw a line down the middle, and title the left side "Current Outlook." Now, record your answers to the previous three questions. Next, title the right side "New Outlook." Use this section to note any changes in your current outlook as you progress through this book. It's important to capture these changes in outlook as a measurement of growth. (I strongly encourage *you to make this a journal entry if you keep a journal. If you don't have a journal, then start one. It will help; trust me!*)

These are the types of questions many of us struggle with, particularly in our younger years, when we find ourselves overwhelmed as we stand in this big field of life (the world), wondering what we are supposed to be doing, which direction we should take, how to know if it's the right decision, etc. These thoughts derive from a longing for purpose; however, oftentimes, we don't realize this because this longing gets contaminated by a false picture of success and the pressure to obtain it.

I would like to help set you free from this vicious cycle. I know firsthand how unhealthy life can become when one gives in to a false mentality regarding the definition of success. Doing so develops a sense of pressure that can easily lead to high levels of anxiousness rooted in fear of the unknown, followed by the hopelessness that accompanies it. Before long, our circumstances begin to torment, whispering in our minds lies such as, *You are not valuable*, or, *You will never succeed*. In order to drown out this voice, many of us fill the void with pleasure or the pursuit of material possessions, or we suffocate the voice with substances that distract our minds—all with the purpose of curing this longing, yet avoiding the questions that force us to search internally.

If any of this sounds like you, I have good news. Success is a mentality. Much more than what you do or achieve, success is who you are! It's the reason you are here! You were created to succeed. My hope is that as you read this book you will begin to see your true self, transforming your outlook on your value, as you assess the deepest levels of your purpose and potential. Success is truly your destiny!

My hope is that as you read this book you will begin to see your true self, transforming your outlook on your value, as you assess the deepest levels of your purpose and potential.

HOW TO NAVIGATE THIS BOOK

It's important to note that while the purpose of this book is personal development strategy, I want you to be aware that everything you read is from a biblical perspective. Faith is the foundation of my life; therefore, everything I produce carries the image and influence of Jesus Christ. The principles are what I consider truth. I've tested them in my life, and so have many others. You don't have to be a Christ-follower to gain great value from these pages; however, I do want to be clear on where all the principles, insight, and strategy derive. Before casting it out as a religious echo chamber, I challenge you to put into practice just one of the principles. Then, measure the impact and results in your life. I assure you that you will not be disappointed.

In this book, I will walk you through *The Mentality of Success* framework. This framework will help you identify a greater sense of purpose and define success for your life. I want to be up-front with you, though. It's important to establish that all four of these zones will require work! This book was never intended to simply be read; its intention serves more to guide. It's a roadmap meant to help you, journey with you. While reading, it is perfectly normal to find yourself putting it down as you wrestle with the exercises or search out answers to questions you never considered before. There is no time limit or pressure here; this is about your value, the greatness within you—so take your time. *The key is that you put into action the wisdom within these pages.*

Accomplishing this will grant you the hope that life often lacks, fulfillment that, like a rare gem, can be hard to find, peace that surpasses the understanding of your friends and neighbors as they continue to follow borrowed mentalities, a strong sense of direction concerning your life purpose along with advice on how to unpack this great assignment in practical ways, and many other benefits! Commit to working through the zones; commit to sticking with this book. If you do so, I am confident that you will begin to experience the life you were created to live. If you're still on the fence, consider the following story.

Timothy and the Dream Box

Dreams require searching. There once was a little boy named Timothy who lived in a world where gold was represented in the form of dreams. In order to realize these dreams, though, little Timmy would have to visit the Dream Maker. The day arrived when little Timmy got to see the dream maker, and boy, was he excited to finally receive his dreams!

When he arrived, he was quickly signed in and given a medium-sized box with images on the outside of all the wonderful places little Timmy's golden dreams would take him. He was filled with joy as he admired this amazing imagery. The detail, the colors, and the flavor inspired his heart with hope for the future.

Wasting no time, little Timmy clutched the dream box under his arm, rushing home as fast as his little legs could take him, ever so careful with this great gift. Storming into the house and upstairs to his room, smiling ear to ear, finally making it to his bed, little Timmy opened the box. Then, he came to a horrific realization. The box, as beautiful as it was on the outside, was only filled with sand on the inside! No gold!

Oh, how disappointed little Timmy was as he sat on his bed, head down, face long, feeling hopeless. All the excitement and anticipation for this moment were completely shattered. He thought to himself, *Without this gold, what am I to do now?* Up until this point, his plan was to spend the rest of his life pursuing and living off his golden dreams. Without the golden dreams, he felt despair, lost, and unsure of where to go or what to do next.

In anger, little Timmy stood up and threw the box on a top shelf in his closet, bitterly vowing never to revisit it again. Instead, he turned his attention to considering how he could still have those dreams: *I just have to figure out how to get the gold in a different way,* little Timmy thought to himself. The years passed by, and little Timmy (who now just went by Tim) grew older and older; however, he never got rid of the box.

Eventually, Tim found a job that would provide for his needs—a well-paying job, one that Tim felt blessed to have. But every now and then, he would think back to the dreams on that once vibrant—but now faded—box.

More years went by, and Tim reached seventy years of age. At that point, he decided it was finally time to get rid of the many keepsakes he'd held onto throughout the years, starting with the now-forgotten dream box. There it sat, still occupying space at the top of an old closet. Tim grabbed a ladder and proceeded to take down the box. Unfortunately, being older in age, Tim struggled to handle the weight of the heavy sand-filled dream box. As he began to remove the box, it slipped out of his hands, dropping onto the tile floor, exploding open from the force, and spilling sand everywhere!

Extremely frustrated at this point, Tim began marching down the ladder to clean this mess. As he reached the bottom, something caught his eye. Tim slowly stepped down from the ladder and began walking towards the foreign objects that lay there in the sand. As Tim got closer to the objects, he realized what he was looking at. There, mixed in with the sand, Tim noticed the golden coins! All this time the gold was there. For years, everything he needed to accomplish his vivid and vibrant dreams sat there underneath the surface of the sand!

Oh, no! Tim said to himself, realizing that, all this time, he could've lived out the dreams in this now-faded box. For the rest of his life, Tim sat there on that floor, reflecting on the time wasted, simply because he never searched through the sand-filled dream box.

This is what happens when we leave dreams unsearched. The dream and discovery zones are the seasons where we search and dig through the sand of our lives. They're where we uncover dreams that add value to our lives and the lives of others. They're where we discover the gold! This gold serves as the resource that will help us accomplish the great dreams and purpose our life was meant for. The next two chapters are all about committing to the dig and searching through that sand-filled box known as your life. Doing so will help you identify all the wonderful gold hidden inside you.

The second section of this book is designed to take you step by step through the process of defining success for your life. It is important that you take your time with this section. Make sure you don't just read through these chapters, but intently focus on applying the knowledge. It is important to spend some time explaining what I mean here. The old myth about habit-building suggested that it takes only twenty-one days to form a new habit. If you are someone who has believed this to be true, I regret to inform you that this is not true. It actually takes up to *sixty-one* days to truly form a new habit.

You are more than worth the time, energy, effort, and maybe even some potential frustration, as you confront some challenging questions.

I think it would be wise of you to keep this truth in mind while applying the knowledge ahead because executing the habits and exercises mentioned all throughout this book will require commitment, focus, and overall, work! Don't shy away from this; you are more than worth the time, energy, effort, and maybe even some potential frustration, as you confront some challenging questions. Stick with it; know that it's perfectly normal to spend 15 to 30 days on one habit, knowledge application, or exercise in each section before moving on to the next point. That's the goal, so again, don't shy away from this vital work.

Now, if you're thinking to yourself, *Joshua, that's crazy!* bear with me. Remember my previous point. This is not intended to be just another book on your reading list. This is more of a guide which means it is meant to be meditated on, searched, wrestled with, put down, and then picked back up once you're ready to move forward. This book is meant to *travel with you* on your journey not simply point you in the right direction.

As Timothy grew older, he could've used a guide like this one. Maybe he would've received encouragement to search through the sand of his life. This book will not only help you do that, but it will also give you guidance on how to further discover the great value within you, develop that value, and then use the results as a guideline for every decision you make moving forward in your life. Get ready! This is the beginning of identifying the purpose and success your life was meant to experience. Let's begin with searching through your dream box.

CHAPTER 1

DREAMS

DREAMS ARE VISIONS WITHOUT SIGHT.

One of the greatest challenges in life is learning how to search and assess which dreams are worth your most precious currency, time. There are moments that can mark our lives forever. Sometimes, this can happen in subtle ways. For me, this took place while attending a leadership conference where the keynote speaker for the day stood and spoke these words as his opening line: "Your imagination is God's whiteboard." Honestly, from that point forward, I can't recall anything else he said. I was still stuck at the opening line.

One of the greatest challenges in life is learning how to search and assess which dreams are worth your most precious currency, your time.

I remember sitting there, putting my head down, and grappling with this truth. I had heard of moments like these before; they were referred to as paradigm shifts which occur when a person experiences a fundamental change in approach or thinking. There is no other explanation that can describe what took place within me in that moment other than a gigantic paradigm shift. It was like something exploded within me. How validated does one feel when they realize that their wild dreams have been affirmed and written by the Creator of the universe? The Creator of the universe activates some of His greatest work through your dreams! I'd say that makes you extremely valuable. I hope this point alone causes a seismic paradigm shift in your mind and heart. If not, though, keep reading!

SALT OF THE WORLD

You are the salt of the earth. But what good is salt if it has lost its flavor? The salt I'm referring to here represents all the value within you. In the ancient world, salt was very valuable: the Greeks thought it contained something almost divine. In fact, if you've ever wondered where the phrase "not worth your salt" originated, it was based on the Romans who sometimes paid their soldiers with salt. A soldier who didn't carry out his duties "was not worth his salt." You, however, are worth every grain of the salt (value) placed within you!

Have you ever seen one of those clear glass salt shakers? Think about how many grains make up this perforated, flavor-filled container. Much like this container, you are also filled with salt, value that gives everything around you flavor. You are a seasoning agent. In a sense, your life adds a distinctive flavor, a specific value, to all of life around you.

One of the many grains of salt that adds flavor to life is your dreams. Why are dreams so important? Because the dreams placed inside of your heart have the ability to provide a very important flavor to your world. If that's not exciting enough, think about this: the dreams within you that carry the highest value not only add flavor (value) to your world, but they also impact the world of those around you!

If you're wondering how or what this flavor looks and feels like, take a look at the following list of flavors dreams can contribute to your life and the lives of others. Your dreams provide:
- → Hope
- → Purpose (future)
- → Identity
- → Belonging
- → Growth

Hope is where life begins! Purpose gives us something to look forward to and be excited about. Identity involves knowing not only who we are but Whose we are. Belonging leads us into relationships that further enhance the flavors of our lives. And growth is the ever so satisfying feeling of engaging our God-given potential. These are the flavors that give life a sense of meaning, that add a vibrant color to your day, creating a sense of urgency and positive outlook on how valuable you are and why you were placed here on this earth. These flavors grant a deeper access to life—real life! The kind that feels totally worth living and enduring, the kind of life that isn't buried by circumstances, but is driven by a contagious sense of purpose. The opposite is true as well. When these flavors are absent, our lives are in danger of becoming colorless. The result is our settling for simple existence rather than an intentional, purpose-filled life.

Hope is where life begins!

When Salt Loses Flavor

When our dreams lose flavor, we accept existing instead of living. Existence is simply living without purpose. This is a dangerous place to be. Many of us have either experienced or witnessed this state: gloomy, unfulfilled, colorless days, accompanied by a lack of motivation or sense of urgency for life. An acceptance that our life was meant for nothing more than our circumstances, our struggles, reflects the low perception of our value and purpose. Does this sound familiar? Have you ever felt or witnessed this state of being? It's a very sad place that I know all too well because I have been there.

Don't Forfeit Your Purpose

I lost my flavor during a season of my life where I developed a false mentality regarding success. I didn't know who I was, the value within me, or much less, how to gain a return on that value. I distinctly remember growing up seeking validation and praise based on silly measures such as how many girls I could attract attention from at once, how stylish my clothes were, how athletic, good looking, dominant, or rich I was ("hood-rich" that is), etc. You see, this false mentality of success never evolved out of its immature, fragile, egotistical roots. I carried this mentality all the way to college, obtaining quite the proficiency, until I was forced to face the incurable longing bubbling up on the inside.

At the time, I felt like I was constantly attempting to fill a bottomless cup. No matter how much I poured in, I couldn't shake the reality of emptiness that remained. No amount of sex, alcohol, distractions, nothing! Emptiness led to masking while out in public (pretending like life is good or everything was okay) while isolating in pain when alone. It was just me and the loud voice in my head performing death by a thousand cuts, slowly chipping away at any sense of hope I held, suffocating any dreams that generated a spark in my life, and before long, the lack of flavor caught up with me in a major way. It was a dark night in more ways than one, as I sat there on that leather couch with my black spiral notebook in hand, writing a letter to my parents because I didn't think life was worth living anymore. There I sat, isolated, broken, feeling lonely, and stripped of all hope—the spitting image of a life that had somehow lost all its flavor.

One of the most tragic instances in life is when we go to turn on that proverbial switch of hope, and no light generates. So we try again, turning that switch on and off, again and again, yet still nothing. This is what I call the *fading period*. We begin to slowly slip further and further into this dark place, engulfed, overwhelmed by this flavorless, seemingly good-for-nothing life. As I write this, suicide is the second leading cause of death for people ages 10 to 34 years old. That's just the numbers for those who followed through with this incredibly unfortunate act. I would dare say the numbers for suicide ideation (which refers to thinking about, considering, or planning suicide) are even higher. This should alarm us all. Where have the dreams, the flavor, the value for life gone? Those life-filled dreams that once ignited your heart but now fade in the dark, what happened to them, or the better question may be, what is currently happening to those dreams? Your purpose is too great to forfeit!

Your purpose is too great to forfeit!

The unfortunate reality of my story is that it isn't unique from many others who are currently experiencing or have experienced the same. Where my story does carry its own uniqueness, however, is when you think about the book you're reading. Imagine if I would've gone through with this action. You wouldn't be reading this book. I wouldn't be sitting here filled with life and purpose as I write, encouraging you to activate your dreams and be the much-needed salt of the earth. I would have forfeited the opportunity to enjoy incredibly valuable friendships, mentors, and leaders. I would have forfeited the chance to meet my amazing wife, the phenomenal experience of hugging my son for the first time, and the wonderful privilege of fatherhood.

Today, my God-given strengths get to thrive as I add value to the world. I've stood on stages speaking into the lives of today's generation, worked in corporate quarters where my professional expertise is sought after by established executives, doctors, business operational leaders, and more. All these accomplishments and milestones, though, are the results of not forfeiting the purpose my life was meant for and why I'm encouraging you not to forfeit the purpose your life was meant for.

We often borrow definitions of success from a false mentality using criteria the world around us has created. As a result, we end up just borrowing pain. That pain translates into a deep need for validation, feelings of insecurity, and many other unhealthy characteristics, all resulting from not searching your own life and discovering what makes you uniquely valuable to this world. The search is what develops your mentality of what it truly means to become a success.

Had I tapped out that night on that couch, I would have missed out, I would have completely forfeited the golden opportunity of contributing flavor to this world and discovering and sharing all the great value I've been entrusted with. The same is true for your life and your dreams! To settle for existence, to allow the dreams within you to die, dishonors the value placed within you, forfeiting your great purpose.

Consider this. What if the dreamers of this world had forfeited their purpose: notable names such as Martin Luther King Jr., Walt Disney, Harriet Tubman, Eleanor Roosevelt, Oprah Winfrey, and Robert Kennedy to names that may be a bit unfamiliar such as Cheick Camara, Ermias Tadesse, Dr. Charles Drew, Katherine Johnson, Thurgood Marshall, Margaret Lee (my grandmother), and the list goes on! One thing all these people have in common with you and me is that their greatness started from the golden dreams within them. Our dreams are important to our being. As Napoleon Hill says: "Cherish your visions and dreams as they are the children of your soul, the blueprints of your ultimate achievements."

What would happen if every soul awakened with the power to take the first step towards achieving their dreams?

Envision this. What would happen if every soul awakened with the power to take the first step towards achieving their dreams? How would this impact families, communities, and the world at large? Or let's scale this back down to your life for a second. How would your life change if you could articulate the valuable dreams you have within you, then awaken those dreams by taking the first step towards achieving? How would your life change? What impact would this have on your sense of purpose and excitement for life? Who would benefit the most from you accomplishing those dreams?

Don't worry about answering right now, but begin allowing questions like these to resonate within your mind and being because here's what I believe and know to be true about you. The value that God placed inside of you is meant to impact your life and the lives of those around you! Read the previous line again, then again, and then one more time until it sticks! It has to stick because if it doesn't, nothing else in this section, or this book for that matter, will serve its intended purpose: which is to help you translate those dreams of yours into flavor that will serve you and the world at large, spreading hope, purpose, identity, a sense of belonging, and growth!

The first step in this process is understanding that it will require you to do some searching. This won't be easy—nothing truly worth having ever is—but it will be worth it. Before you can embrace the search, though, you must first accept that the search comes with resistance that often makes embracing the search such a difficult process. This resistance is what I call the *3 Seeds of Limitation*. In an effort to help you overcome these limitations, let's take a moment to acknowledge what they are and how you can leverage each for good in your journey.

3 SEEDS OF LIMITATION

What are also known as self-limiting beliefs, the three seeds of limitation are fear, doubt, and inaction. The moment you decide to do anything great with your life, including exploring those God-given dreams, you can count on one, if not all three, of these seeds to push back on your decision. Have you ever envisioned yourself doing something you knew in your heart would have a great impact on your life and others only to find yourself overcome with paralyzing fear and frustration? Or maybe you never envision yourself doing anything due to the limiting seed of doubt causing you to believe that you could never accomplish something of great value. How about one I know very well: the moments where we know we should move, do, or become, yet we squander away the opportunity due to inaction? All three of these seeds can seem like a bad thing at first; however, I want to challenge your perspective on how to nurture these seeds for good in your life.

Think about what happens when people strengthen their physical body. At some point during the process, they grow stronger because they've pushed their muscles through a certain threshold of resistance, causing growth. Each seed of limitation involves a threshold of resistance. How you push through this resistance leads to one of two potential growth paths. One path grows into greater limitation (negative) while the alternative path causes the seed to experience positive growth, adding good to your life. Consider the following examples.

Fear
The seed of fear grows in one of two ways. Either this seed sprouts into more limiting fear in your life, preventing you from ever growing

those God-given dreams, or this seed sprouts into the alternative which is courage!

Here's a simple yet common example how this often plays out. Have you ever wanted to accomplish a goal that was valuable and important to you only to realize you have no idea where to even start? Not knowing produces the seed of fear creating resistance between where you are and where you want to be. At this point, you have a choice of how this seed grows. The path of greater limitation is fixating over the fact that you don't know how you will accomplish this goal in your current state, so you instead choose to rehearse every worst-case scenario, validating your fear, and never trying to accomplish anything. The alternative path is accepting that most, if not all, great things begin at "I don't know." This seed of fear caused by the unknown is just an opportunity to push through the resistance and grow the level of courage necessary to go after it! How you water this seed determines how it grows. How are you watering the seed of fear in your life?

How you water this seed determines how it grows. How are you watering the seed of fear in your life?

Doubt

The seed of doubt grows in one of two ways. Either this seed sprouts into more limiting doubt, causing anxious self-defeating thoughts about you and your future to replay over and over, or this seed sprouts into the alternative which is clarity (of self and future).

Here's an example of how this often plays out. Have you ever struggled to believe after experiencing the bitter sting of failure? You start off with positive expectations, yet the moment you are faced with adversity, you begin to seriously doubt yourself? At this point, you have the choice to determine how this seed of doubt grows. The path of greater limitation is you destroying your self-image by replaying damaging thoughts about yourself and your abilities, growing this seed into a pessimistic outlook on your future and everything around you. The alternative path is possessing a clear understanding of who you are, what you're made of, and how you best serve. This provides the necessary clarity to silence the negative inner talk, growing your seed of doubt into clear vision. How you water this seed determines how it grows. How are you watering the seed of doubt in your life?

Inaction

The seed of inaction also grows in one of two ways. Either this seed sprouts into more limiting inaction, causing you to waste all the great value within you, or this seed sprouts into the alternative, which is accessing more of your potential.

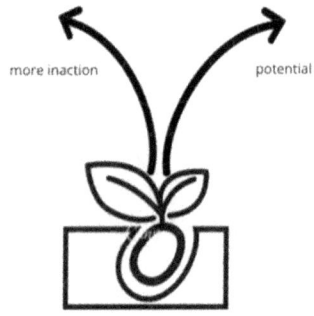

Here's an example of how this plays out. You know exactly the direction you need to focus your attention, yet for some strange reason, you don't! At this point, you have the choice to determine how this seed of inaction grows in your life. The path of greater limitation is to continue wasting time, squandering away all the great value you've been given. The alternative path, however, is recognizing that your potential is too valuable; therefore, it must not be wasted. You tune your ear to the urgent call within your heart, realizing that others can benefit from the greatness within you. As a result, this realization leads to greater action, growing the seed of inaction into greater levels of your potential. How you water this seed determines how it grows. How are you watering the seed of inaction in your life?

Hopefully you now understand that these three seeds are a natural part of life. How you grow these seeds is the deciding factor of how they will impact your life. Before you embrace the search that we will discuss in the upcoming section, you first have to accept that you will be faced with resistance at every step of this journey. Don't let this truth deter you; it's all a part of what will shape your experience and cause tremendous growth in your life. Yes, the challenging news is that these seeds never disappear completely. The good news is that you can overcome this challenge and transform these seeds of limitation into good, causing them to serve as seeds of success in your life.

> **You can overcome this challenge and transform these seeds of limitation into good, causing them to serve as seeds of success in your life.**

Now that you understand the two alternative paths, as you search through your God-given dreams, be courageous when faced with the resistance of fear. Trust that the unclear areas in your life and vision will gain greater clarity. And finally, defeat the inaction that's robbing you of the opportunity to access deeper levels of your potential. If you do these, you will elevate your experience of this important search.

EMBRACING THE SEARCH

Have you ever completed a word search puzzle—the one that involves a box filled with what appear to be random letters that you must search through to find the hidden words? Word search puzzles are usually fun, engaging, and often viewed as a cool brain exercise that even have the ability to bring out our competitiveness at times. It's safe to say we generally hold a positive outlook on word search puzzles, even though they require that we search intently through a box filled with letters, so that we may discover all the words hidden on the inside.

Before, I told you that your dreams represent salt; well, each grain of salt is like a word search puzzle. The random letters of your dreams are the uncertainties you have when trying to decide what your dreams mean for your life, which dreams are worth pursuing, and how you will ultimately accomplish them. Much like the hidden words among the random letters in a word search, there are hidden direction, purpose, desires, and connections, all within your dreams. In other words, just like the answers are already inside that word search puzzle, know that the answers are already inside of your dreams. You just have to search for them!

APPLIED VISION

A vision without a plan is just a dream. The reason the search is so important is because this process will help clear out the fog, transforming your dreams into clear vision. Vision is the clarity of knowing what your dreams mean for your life, which dreams are worth pursuing, and most importantly, how to organize the pursuit of your dreams. Once you've determined which dreams are worth going after and when you should pursue them, you will then be prepared to overcome the challenges that commonly prevent us from developing a plan for accomplishing those dreams.

This is what I like to call *dream stewardship*. We will get to how you can develop a plan later. For now, focus your attention on how to overcome the challenges mentioned earlier. The two challenges we encounter the most when developing a plan for our dreams are deciphering the types of dreams we hold and prioritizing our dreams by value and impact. This is important because, as we read earlier, our most precious currency is time. Knowing which dreams deserve the greatest investment of your time is a huge step in gaining a return on the salt (value) within you. Beginning with the first challenge, which is to better understand the dreams we hold, let's explore the 5 Dream Types.

THE 5 DREAM TYPES

These five dream types will help you search and attribute value to your dreams. The goal here is to prioritize your dreams, so you can determine and manage how much time you dedicate to the dreams you hold. I want to emphasize this point because, far too often, we accept the idea that we can only pursue one dream. For instance, someone who really wants to be a singer may invest their entire life into pursuing that dream (nothing wrong with this); however, there may be additional dreams that this singer never searched for that would've added just as much, if not even more, value to their life than the dream to be a singer.

I guess what I'm suggesting here is that you pour out ALL THE VALUE! Leave not a single contribution to this world within; pour all of your potential out! List all your dreams, every single one of them, so that you will better understand the types of dreams you hold. Once you increase your understanding, then you will be able to prioritize which dreams to pursue. The table below provides a snapshot of each dream type along with the challenges and benefits of each. For more in-depth explanations and examples, be sure to carefully read through the full description of each dream type. I will be using my life as an example to explain each dream type.

Leave not a single contribution to this world within; pour all of your potential out!

---

5 Types of Dreams	Definition	Benefits	Challenges
Fairy Tale	These dreams aren't rooted in anything "real."	They help people develop a great imagination.	They short-circuit purpose.
Seasonal	These dreams have an expiration date.	They help people gain experience and clarify their direction.	They can cause large letdowns.
Material	These dreams are centered around obtaining things.	They help people obtain rewards that boost motivation.	They increase your thirst for things and dehydrate your purpose.
Shared	These are connected dreams.	They help people build lifelong friendships and provide company on the journey.	They're not really your dream, and pursuing them can cause resentment.
Service	These dreams focus on serving and impacting others.	They help people build and leave a legacy.	They require investment and growth.

Fairy Tale Dreams

When I was a little boy, I wanted to be a Teenage Mutant Ninja Turtle! Now, before you laugh, I need you to know that this was a real thing. Another dream I held close was my belief that if I tried hard enough, I could fly! All I needed to do was tie a towel around my neck and run through our family trailer as fast as I could, over and over, jumping off my parents' furniture for an extra boost. (As you can imagine, my mother wasn't too fond of this dream.) I also had an imaginary Batman utility belt that gave me all the help I would ever need: the ability to freeze time, make the girl in my elementary class like me, become invisible, you know, the basic stuff.

These dreams were real to me at the time; however, the truth is, these were all fairy tale dreams, not rooted in anything "real." I hate to break it to you, but chemically enhanced turtles with super ninja skills (acquired from a large chemically enhanced rat) don't exist! For me though, this dream felt so real, I could close my eyes and literally see these things come to life! Before you get too far ahead of me, you need to understand that this type of dream, as childish as it may seem, isn't all bad. Take a look at some of the challenges and benefits of fairy tale dreams.

Benefits

Fairy tale dreams may seem childlike on the surface, but they help us develop a wonderful imagination. Some of the world's greatest inventions, attractions, and ideas started out as fairy tale-type dreams! Did you know the Nobel Prize-worthy discovery of insulin, which helps keep people struggling with diabetes alive, literally started off as a fairy tale dream? Walt Disney World . . . fairy tale dream. The movie *Avatar* (one of my favorites) . . . fairy tale dream. The periodic table . . . yep, you guessed it, fairy tale dream. The sewing machine, video games, books, and so much more, represent men and women across the world who, in their imaginations, created solutions that saved lives, impacted communities, and provided major contributions to this world. My point is, don't let the name of this dream type undermine its value.

Just because this dream type is often not rooted in anything "real," doesn't mean it can't produce real value. It absolutely can; searching and understanding this dream type helps us figure out how to translate the fairy tale into real value. You may be wondering how to do this. Well, the key word here is *value*. Think about many of the fairy tales I mentioned previously; what do they all have in common? They all center around adding positive value to the world. If your dream isn't "real," yet you believe it carries valuable insight, inspiration, or hope, then I'd say that's a dream worth exploring. Ask yourself the following question: *How could this fairytale dream be produced into a tangible asset?* Could it be through a drawing, a physical product, or software? Maybe a movie, song, or invention. The options are nearly endless. I encourage you to search and dream up the possibilities.

Challenges

The greatest challenge with fairy tale dreams is that they can short-circuit your purpose. Back in college, when I was single and ready to mingle, I used to work within the college services sector on campus. My role was in student services as a peer educator. One day, we had a new team member join us, whom we will name Ash for confidentiality's sake. I thought Ash was a very pretty young woman, one I was excited to get to know during her onboarding. When the time came for her to get acclimated to our team and department, guess who was selected to train and walk Ash through the onboarding process? Yep, you guessed it, I was! I thought to myself, *This must be the matchmaking hand of God, right?* Well, this thought was short-lived.

One day, while we sat at the front desk, I noticed the traffic in the office had died down, presenting a great opportunity for small talk. I saw this as a chance to get to know her a bit better, so I decided to spark up a conversation. Considering that we both were college students, I thought it would be an appropriate question, so I asked Ash what her dreams and plans were for the future. I couldn't believe what happened next. I kid you not; she looked up at me with the most serious face and proceeded to inform me that her "big dream" in life was to marry someone rich and ride off into the sunset on a white horse, and, no, I'm not exaggerating. I asked about the horse (all I could hear in that moment was . . . run!).

As you can imagine, I was in utter disbelief, not to mention totally no longer interested—not because there's anything wrong with marrying rich. (If you can pull it off, go for it!) Instead, I recognized the dangerous side of this fairy tale dream. A fairy tale dream is dangerous when it short-circuits your purpose. There's nothing wrong with marrying rich, but if you think your entire existence is to arrive comfortably and safely at the end of life, you are short-circuiting all the great value within you! Furthermore, a dream that isn't connected to anything real and doesn't require hard work is a dangerous fairy tale. I encourage you to run from such dreams! Burn them! These types of dreams are not worth a second of your time.

Seasonal Dreams

As I grew older, my dreams grew to be more seasonal. There was a time in my life when my dream was to become an NBA basketball player. I can recall long nights, staying outside in the driveway getting up hundreds of shots, working on the left-hand layup, perfecting the offhand dribble, envisioning myself hitting game-winning shots, and getting a return on the athleticism I'd been blessed with. This dream was also packaged with another dream of wanting to one day become a music producer. I loved writing music that impacted the lives of others. Piecing together ensembles moved my heart emotionally and sparked inspiration within my soul!

The thing about these particular dreams is that they were supported with skill and talent. Back in high school, at five-foot-nine, I could drop-step and dunk the basketball on a ten foot rim. I was quick, coordinated, and all the athletic foundational blocks that might suggest a possible future in a sport. When it came to music, the natural talent and skill were also there. I learned how to play piano by ear just by listening to my mother play. I would hear melodies and musical compilations in my mind that I had the ability to then produce. Lyrics would move my heart and the hearts of others when I would share them. I just knew, at that time, that this is what I was meant to do for the rest of my life!

Now, I'm not suggesting that these thoughts weren't true, but I am suggesting that there were things about these seasonal dreams that I didn't know at the time. I didn't know that just because you possess a natural talent for something, it doesn't mean you will necessarily be doing that thing for the rest of your life. Seasonal dreams have an expiration date. Over the years, I've learned a lot about this type of dream. Understanding the following benefits and challenges of seasonal dreams may help you put this dream type into proper perspective.

Benefits

So, I never made it to the NBA (shocker), and, while I have written many songs and even had one gain placement on a mainstream album release, I never became the famous singer/performer I thought I wanted to be. What if I told you that none of the results I just mentioned actually mattered, though? What if these dreams were never about accomplishing the results I had in mind? What if all the time I invested in getting up shots, working on perfecting my game, writing song after song, melody after melody, or the hours I spent breaking my neck, producing music on that little XP computer, trying to get closer to my dream, weren't actually about the dream itself?

Here's what I mean. While seasonal dreams do have an expiration date, their purpose does not expire. Think about this. Sure, I never became an NBA player, but I did gain a significant amount of experience in developing discipline, work ethic, passion, friendships, opportunities to travel and see the world outside my little box! Writing and producing music helped develop my creative side and allowed me an opportunity to practice growing in my ability to communicate and connect with people—both skills I use to provide for my family today and, dare I say, the foundation for writing the very book you're reading.

That's the benefit of seasonal dreams. It's usually never about the dream itself; it's about gaining experience and clarifying direction. During this season of my life, when I wasn't quite sure how my future would unfold, these dreams led me in the direction I was supposed to go, helping me to gain experiences that would benefit me for the rest of my life. Have you ever seen one of those lanterns used to gently light up a path or walkway? Seasonal dreams often serve us in the same way those little guiding lights do during times when we lack clarity of what lies ahead or when thinking about the future feels like traveling down a dark road. In these seasons of life, this type of dream helps provide just enough light to make it to the next step, granting us a sense of direction and great opportunities to gain valuable experience.

Challenges

Let's be honest, though. Sometimes when seasonal dreams expire, if we're not careful, they will take a piece of us with them. The challenge with seasonal dreams is that these dreams can cause a major letdown when their purpose is not understood. Take, for instance, my desire to be a pro ballplayer. On graduation day, when it became quite evident no one would be reaching out and granting me a scholarship to play ball, that dream officially expired. Here's what could have happened: I could have expired along with this dream.

If we think about it, we've seen this happen before. We know people who are still in the same place doing the same thing they were doing when we last saw them in high school because all the dreams they once held expired. After experiencing such an expiration, many of us get stuck in the place I call the *letdown*, and sadly, some never recover. This is the greatest challenge with seasonal dreams. This massive letdown is caused when we lack the proper perspective of a seasonal dream's purpose. Far too often we associate our value with the dream instead of seeing the dream for the salt that it is.

Just because a seasonal dream expires DOES NOT mean your life expires along with it!

Understand me clearly here. Just because a seasonal dream expires DOES NOT mean your life expires along with it! There's so much more salt (value) within you! If it feels like certain dreams have expired, don't fret; instead, consider the purpose and value these dreams attributed to your life. Even as expired dreams, they can still have value. The key is to extract that value and use it for good as you move forward. Questions like, *What skills, growth, or development, have I gained from pursuing this dream?*

and *How can I apply this moving forward?* are really good to consider as you approach the expiration date of this dream type.

Material Dreams

I eventually admitted to myself why I really wanted to play professional ball. Yes, I did have a passion for the competitive portion and a bit of athleticism to leverage, but let's be serious; it takes a whole lot more than that to make it to the NBA. Let's pretend though, that I was actually good enough to get there. How much would I have enjoyed that job? Now that I've invested so much into searching and growing myself, I can tell you without a doubt, I would NOT have enjoyed that job! Traveling from city to city, spending multiple weeks a year away from my loved ones, having to pick up and move my family across the country at a moment's notice, and other challenges that come with that world just aren't very appealing to me. (What can I say? I'm a homebody country boy.) I don't value those things much at all. The more I searched this dream, I began to realize that this was a material dream. In other words, I really only wanted this dream for the money!

Material dreams are centered around obtaining *things*: money, cars, clothes, luxury homes, expensive trips, fame. You name that thing, and it's most likely on the list. I grew up in a poor town where you don't know a lot of people who have the material means to enjoy the previously mentioned list. While growing up back in Immokalee, Florida, I only knew of one famous athlete from my hometown by the name of Edgerrin James. He made it to the NFL and earned himself a really nice living. While in high school, I got to visit his home—and, boy, was it beautiful! I stood in that neighborhood checking out all the other big homes in the neighborhood, thinking to myself that one day I wanted the same for me and my family. I realized later on that experiences like this one drove my material dream of making it to the NBA. I figured if I could make it there, I could have the things he had, the things I dreamed of possessing.

It's important to note that there's nothing wrong with material dreams. I, to this day, still have material dreams that I will accomplish. Like the other dream types, though, there are some benefits and challenges to material dreams. Let's take a look.

Benefits

Many psychological studies analyze the power of reward systems. Rewards typically serve as reinforcers. When we demonstrate a certain behavior, rewards increase the probability that we will repeat that behavior in order to receive another positive reinforcement (reward). The point is that material dreams almost always involve obtaining rewards that boost our motivation, affirm our behavior, and increase our esteem or sense of positive progress. This is a good thing.

The first car I ever bought with my own money required months of discipline and hard work, all behavioral-based actions. I had to demonstrate a certain behavior to raise enough cash to purchase that beautiful Honda I still own today! The reward (new car) is what served as the reinforcement for my behavior change and consistency. This is a great benefit of material dreams. Having a proverbial light or reward at the end of the tunnel can often serve as the driving force that causes us to adopt key behavioral changes in our habits, work ethic, focus, resilience, and consistency. Look at all the value a material dream can produce!

This dream type sometimes gets a bad rap, however, because it's often associated with money-hunger and greed. I believe this dream type to be the most misunderstood of the five dream types. Let me say this loud and clear: there is nothing wrong with pursuing material-based dreams! These dreams can spark intrinsic motivation, helping to create a fun system in your life that can be greatly rewarding in more ways than one. If you have material dreams, be sure to leverage them in this way, and you will reap the benefits.

Challenges

The greatest challenge with material dreams is if this dream type is not tamed with discipline, it can negatively increase your thirst for things while draining purpose from your life. The number of people in this world who gained a massive number of material items (many we would all love to have) yet, in the process, lost their souls is well documented. Their soul being their sense of purpose in life. In other words, there is absolutely no benefit to material gain when you are left empty inside. I call this *dehydrated purpose*.

Dehydrated purpose occurs when we spend so much time and energy gaining things that we forget to feed the most valuable areas of our being—the areas that matter most, that keep our minds strong, our hearts and motives pure, and ultimately, guard our soul. This sounds intense, I know, but it's true. I would say material dreams are the second most dangerous for this reason. This dream type can hypnotize, distracting our attention towards the shiny things; meanwhile, there's a thief with a life-sized vacuum sucking the vitality out of life's most important things . . . our character, our leadership ability, our time with loved ones and family . . . you know, the stuff that actually matters!

> **A thief with a life-sized vacuum can suck the vitality out of life's most important things . . . our character, our leadership ability, our time with loved ones and family . . . you know, the stuff that actually matters!**

It's important that in the pure-hearted pursuit of material dreams, we don't lose sight of the more important aspects of life. Great indicators that this dream type has gone sour can be found when you have much in possessions, yet you have no joy, peace, ability to demonstrate kindness, ability to love or be loved, patience, goodness, or self-control, among other qualities. Pay attention to these signs, and if you find yourself experiencing these challenges, it may be a good idea to reset this dream. You may need to part ways with some of the materials for a while to materially detox and rehydrate your purpose!

Shared Dreams

When it was time for me to head off to college, I didn't have to endure the stress that many seniors experience while making this tough transition. The reason for this lack of stress is that I had the privilege of experiencing this shift with my best friend Ramces. He and I have been blessed with an incredible friendship for over twenty-plus years.

I remember the first time I met Ramces. It was the first day of middle school during the lunch hour. There I was sitting at a table full of strangers, quietly eating my lunch when, all of a sudden, music began to blast. I heard some kid's voice begin to sing over the PA system. All the students rose to their feet in amazement, and there he was . . . the Haitian Justin Bieber himself, Ramces! Later that day, he and I met in chorus class (which—fun fact—I dreaded attending because I thought I would get made fun of for singing), and since then, Ramces and I have been inseparable.

I point out this friendship in order to draw your attention to the power of a shared dream. This dream type is very special! Like all dream types, though, this one has its benefits and challenges. Let's explore them.

Benefits

Shared dreams grant us the opportunity to pursue a dream with someone else or connect our dream to someone else's. With this dream type, we experience lifelong friendships that serve as great company on our journey towards accomplishing our dreams. It's a win-win situation! Honestly, even if you don't accomplish the dream, look at the eternal value you gain from experiencing life with a rare friend.

Shared dreams, more than any other type, are much more about the journey than the actual dream. I can't put into words all the memories, laughter, and fun Ramces and I have experienced throughout the years. The milestones we've reached, the hard times we've supported each other through, all of this opportunity sparked because of our shared love and dream for music and purpose. That's where our shared dream began. Now it has blossomed into over two decades (and counting) of salt and flavor added to both of our lives. Think about how incredible that is! That's why this dream type is unique.

Challenges

The greatest challenges with shared dreams are the moments when the dreams aren't actually shared! I like to split this into two categories: pressure and sacrifice.

1) Pressure: There have been many people who have pursued a dream that wasn't actually their own: doctors who went to medical school because mom and dad said this was the best choice, lawyers who are miserable as they move from case to case feeling unfulfilled and robbed of what their real dream was, etc. Maybe, as you read this, you realize that you, too, are carrying a dream that you thought you shared but now realize that this dream never belonged to you. This can be a very lonely and frustrating place. I encourage you to seek out someone you trust to talk through this challenge. Don't look for solutions initially; just talk through why you don't share this dream and where your heart really is and why.

2) Sacrifice: Many people will share a dream with someone just because they want to see that person accomplish their dream, not because it's their own. An important point to make here is that there is nothing wrong with sharing a dream with someone because you want to see them succeed. This means you are committing to a short-term or long-term sacrifice. Both can be admirable.

Bitterness, like weeds in between the cracks of pavers on your back patio, can grow uncontrolled.

A short-term sacrifice is when your goal is to help someone reach a certain outcome before returning to your own dream. The trouble I often see here, though, is that people sacrifice their dream and never return to it. This leaves an open space where seeds of bitterness can be planted that will eat away at your heart as you become older. Bitterness, like weeds in between the cracks of pavers on your back patio, can grow uncontrolled. (Trust me; I've experienced this firsthand.) Once they have fully invaded the crevasses of your heart, your demeanor may become highly irritable, negative, and cold.

A long-term sacrifice takes place when you completely give up your dream in honor of someone else's. A long-term sacrifice is only admirable when you have truly relinquished all desire for your own dreams. This is a very difficult thing to do and requires a tremendous amount of love, humility, and most of all, purpose. Know that there are often people in our lives who have done this for us. I encourage you to recognize those who have sacrificed their dreams either temporarily to share in helping you accomplish yours or completely in honor of yours. Do not undervalue these people; go out of your way to praise and recognize their contribution. Not many understand the level of sacrifice and heart this requires.

Service Dreams

I believe this to be the most important dream type because it is bigger than you. I'd like to draw your attention back to the beginning of this discussion where I mentioned my love for creating music. Consider the following progression.

What started off as a simple passion for music led to the discovery of a writing skill. I noticed that I could naturally piece thoughts together that touched people's emotions, provoking laughter, tears, or thought.

This skill evolved into discovering an ability to speak. I think back to the day one of my leaders walked up to me and said, "You're speaking next month," I thought he had lost his mind. I had never spoken before besides in my alone time, talking out loud to . . . myself. Yet, the skill was there. This blossomed into training, then coaching, then strategy consulting, before ultimately leading me to become an organizational psychologist.

Looking back, I realize that at the root of all these skills is something much more important. My love for serving people! I never wrote music for myself. I always wrote with others in mind. Early on, it was never about, *How can I make a lot of money doing this?* Every time I sat down to write, sing, or produce, I wondered, *How can I impact the people listening? How can I make them feel something with this rhythm?* or *How can I move their hearts with this melody or lyric*? were always the thoughts at the forefront of my mind. I can vividly remember how these moments would cause my life to explode with flavor!

Today, this service-driven mentality still remains at the center of every dream and thing I do. Whether I'm coaching and training a room full of C-suite executives, providing strategy consults to young professionals, or simply pulling out my voice recorder to jot down a song idea, the mindset remains the same. *How can I serve others the best . . . impact others the most?* Thoughts like these fill my life with a tremendous amount of flavor (value). The reason for this is because of this dream type. Service dreams ignite a flavorful, value-filled return every time, no matter what. Why? Because this is the most powerful and valuable dream one can possess. The service dream type adds more salt, more flavor, than any other dream type. Therefore, I will forever shout this next point from the mountaintop! If you have a service dream, one that's bigger than you, go after it! This dream is of the highest importance because of the wide-ranging impact it has on your life and the lives of those around you.

How can I serve others the best . . . impact others the most?

Eternity is a state outside the realm of time. Therefore, time does not apply to anything that has eternal value. Service is an eternal value. Service ignites eternal consequences (good or bad). Think about the shifts in our history that are directly connected to someone who decided to serve a group of people. Many of these historical figures are no longer with us today, yet the impact of their service lives on. Why? Because service is an eternal value.

This eternal reward not only impacts those on the receiving side, but also those serving. Have you ever been a part of a service project where you got the opportunity to step out into your community and serve those whose circumstances are less fortunate than yours? If you have, you may have felt humbled by the exposure to other people's challenges, giving you a new perspective on life. You may have experienced a small or great boost in your gratitude or an increase of fulfillment from helping someone else. Many have served in this way, and these experiences have left a mark for the rest of their lives.

Think about those on the receiving end. They, too, are marked, oftentimes by strangers they will only meet once, yet they will carry the value that stranger provided for the rest of their lives. Some will even pass this value down to their family and friends for generations. Wow! How incredible is that? That's the power of service. Your service-based dream has the power to leave a lasting impact on the people, places, or things you are meant to serve! Let's further explore the benefits and challenges of this final dream type.

Benefits

Service-based dreams leave a legacy. There's a principle-based law in serving; that principle is the law of giving. Many of the world's richest people will tell you that one of the key practices when looking to build wealth is giving. To the simple mind, this might not make any sense, but it's true! We don't serve to get. Yes, you heard me. I know with millions of businesses, goods, services, and dreams that have turned into very lucrative opportunities, it may sound foolish to think we should seek to serve instead of looking to get something for our service. However, that's *exactly* what I am telling you.

Our lives get to the level that we give first. Here's another way to think about this. The level of flavor and seasoning (value) our life receives is directly correlated to the level of flavor and seasoning we pour out on others. This determines the legacy we will leave. Do you want a life filled with eternal values such as purpose and fulfillment? Then activate a service dream that will make a positive, life-giving impact on those around you.

> **Our lives get to the level that we give first.**

As I mentioned earlier, all I could articulate at first when it came to my dreams and what I wanted to do with my life was that I loved people. I noticed this consistent enjoyment, inspiration, and focus I carried when it came to impacting the lives of others, seeing people grow and experience life at a greater level. This added a tremendous amount of value to my life. It's the sole reason I sit here in the early hours of the morning writing this book. Would I like to sell millions of copies? Absolutely! However, the reason for wanting to sell a million copies is centered around my belief that this book will have a great impact on lives, giving people sense of purpose and helping others define what true success is in life. That's the power of a service-centered dream! My focus must always remain first and foremost on that service point in order to sustain this dream type.

The same is true for you. Your focus on whom your service-based dream will enrich will catapult you towards accomplishing this dream type. It will ultimately build a lasting legacy which only happens when our service extends far beyond our time. Legacy is not about the number of people you reach but rather the size of influence you leave. If your service dream greatly impacts just the people in your immediate circle, that's a legacy that leaves a tremendously valuable influence. That's a service dream, one that I encourage you to spend your time pursuing.

Challenges

This dream type does come with its challenges; although, I will say, this is a great challenge to have. The challenge is growth. Service dreams require growth! This dream type requires more of *who you are*, rather than *what you do*! We must continue developing as leaders, as managers of our priorities, time, and values. This dream type stretches us beyond our comfort zones; it scans the strength of our character for weaknesses that could potentially hurt the people we've been entrusted to serve. It is impossible to accomplish this dream type without committing to intentionally and consistently growing yourself.

Service dreams are not for the weak, not for the half-hearted or self-centered, and surely not for those who don't recognize the great responsibility that comes with this dream type. Service dreams must honor and demonstrate the power of enriching others, call us to higher ground in every area of our lives. A service dream is eternally valuable; it's the Infinity Stone of life (sorry, had to throw one in for my Marvel nerds).

These are good challenges; therefore, the best advice I would give anyone pursuing such a valuable dream is this. Surround yourself with people who will keep the fire burning. This dream type is heavy because it is bigger than you. Oftentimes, service dreams will require you to enlist others to join in and help. That's why growing yourself as a leader is so important. If you're going to accomplish such a dream as this, you will need big hands, the hands of God, accompanied with a community of people who are inspired by your service dream and want to help activate it. Take a moment to think about who around you is inspired by your service dream? Who, in your circle or within your reach, has the skills, talents, strengths, and gifts that can support this dream? If you're struggling a bit to identify these people, ask God to show you who they are, and He will guide you (Psalm 32:8).

Wisdom for Your Search

Now that you understand these five dream types, I hope your life opens up in a fresh way. I hope you feel more equipped to prioritize your dreams according to their value as this will help you determine how to manage your most precious currency, your time. In addition, prioritization also gives our lives a sense of direction, clarity which gives us confidence that we are moving towards purpose, and fulfillment.

Here's a bonus: now that you've gained this great sense of clarity and direction, I want to close this chapter with a few final pieces of wisdom that will help maintain the value of your salt and the flavor of your life.

1) **Assess what truly drives you.**
   Our thoughts have a great impact on our dreams. When was the last time you took a few days (a minimum of seven) to audit what you think about? There was a pivotal moment in my life when I did this and realized I was spending more time thinking about pleasures than values. For instance, I thought about how much money I could make five times as much as the amount of value I could give. This line of thinking, over time, can turn the most valuable dreams hollow and build a thirst for desires that we can never quench because these desires can't satisfy the soul. Search your thoughts to find out where your treasure is. What you treasure will control you. If you treasure adding value (salt) to the world, then this treasure will control your every action, decision, and thought. Identify what drives you.

2) **Pay attention to the similarities and themes of your dreams.**
   Think back to the stories I shared in the 5 Dream Types section. Notice how each dream had little bread crumbs that led to the greater theme of loving people. I then was able to reverse engineer how I demonstrated that love through my skills, strengths, and talents (more on this in the next chapter). What are the common themes you notice within your dreams? Is it a particular group of people you'd like to serve—a specific age, race, or demographic? Do you find that there's a shared goal between dreams? These are a few questions to get you thinking about a potential theme your dreams may be hovering around.

3) **Stay away from the comparison trap!**

   One of the worst things we can do with our God-given dreams is compare them to someone else's. Let's imagine for a second that we both have children (or a puppy, if you prefer). Say I walked up to you and with serious intent said, "Hey, I like your child better. Let's trade!" I wish I could see the look on your face as you consider this ridiculous idea (and if you have difficult kids, and you're responding with "I would definitely trade right now!" . . . stop it!). Just like all children are unique, special, and not to be compared, so are your dreams. To compare the value of your dream to someone else's is to dishonor the value of yours. Dreams are not to be compared. They are to be honored, cherished, and stewarded well with intent.

4) **Measure your dreams by sphere of influence, not number of people.**

   Often, we equate high value to large following. Therefore, if my dream isn't generating a large following, then it must not be valuable enough. Think about the lives that have been forever changed because of a word from a friend or an example set for a child by an older influence, positively marking their life. These aren't instances that involve large numbers, but the influence is enormous. For me, that example is my grandmother, Margaret Lee. *You* most likely have never heard of her, yet her influence is one of the greatest inspirations for this book. Her example and impact will last for the rest of my life and be passed down to my children. That's real influence, legacy, purpose! Don't overlook those within your sphere of influence whose lives you could positively impact for generations. Furthermore, do not abandon the lives your dreams have been assigned to impact; they need your influence!

5) **Be aware of the time horizon test.**

   In a world where immediate gratification is the new drug, developing the patience it takes to see highly valuable dreams accomplished can be tough. That's why this principle is one of the most important principles a person can adopt. My most valuable dreams often have taken five, ten, or fifteen years to finally come to life. This doesn't mean that all dreams take this amount of time, but I would argue that the best and most valuable ones, more often than not, do. This is because the most important part of accomplishing your dreams is not the dream itself but the person you become in the process. Cheap dreams that don't require any growth, sacrifice, or investment of time are hollow and lack flavor. They aren't worth even the smallest increments of your time. Stay committed when the time horizon begins to cause fatigue; your investment will be well worth it in the end. And if you ever find yourself getting discouraged, know that this book took six years to write. When your patience is tested, and you begin to feel discouraged, remember the potentially extended time horizon dreams often require.

By now, I hope that what seemed like random letters in the word search of your dreams and life are starting to piece together a bit. This is just the beginning. Next, we will take this a step further as we begin to unpack more of the boundless value placed within you. Before moving on to the next chapter, be sure to complete the practical application portion of this chapter. This work is extremely important towards getting the greatest return on those dreams of yours. Take your time with these exercises; they may take a few days—maybe even weeks—to complete. That's okay. The key is that you commit to showing up and sticking with it. Value quality over quantity. Know that you will gain an immense amount of clarity by doing the work.

Commit to showing up and sticking with it. Value quality over quantity.

APPLICATION

The following chart is an assessment meant to help you further search, identify, and prioritize your dreams. Keep in mind that service-based dreams are the best dreams to pursue first. Also, notice there aren't any action plan questions listed below. This is on purpose. I don't want you to think about execution just yet or judge your answers, for that matter. Moving too fast through this process can be overwhelming; it can crush your spirit. Simply assess for now by thoughtfully filling out the chart below. There is no time limit or max on this exercise.

Question	Dream 1:	Dream 2:	Dream 3:
What is my dream, and why do I want to accomplish it?			
What type of dream is this?			
Where did this dream originate? What makes me want to pursue it?			
How much of this dream is within my control?			
Whom will this dream impact besides me? How? *Be as specific as possible.*			
What will happen if I don't accomplish this dream? Who will this impact?			
On a day-by-day basis, what am I doing to move closer to this dream?			

REFLECTION

1) What is your greatest takeaway from this chapter?

2) How have your ideas regarding dreams changed since you started reading this chapter?

3) What were the most challenging moments or points in this chapter? What made them so?

4) How did you prioritize your dreams after completing the assessment exercise?

5) How will this prioritization impact your life moving forward?

CHAPTER 2

DISCOVERY

WELCOME TO THE EXPLORATION ZONE! GET YOUR SHOVEL BECAUSE WE'RE ABOUT TO DIG!

Let me just say this right from the start: This is the zone that many people hate. However, I'm going to teach you to love it by removing all of the pressure this zone often creates. Imagine a world where you truly understand you! A world where you know and can clearly articulate all the value within you. Your beliefs, principles, personality type, your strengths, talents, skills, gifts, and more. A world where you not only understand the aforementioned value, but you also have a clear vision on how these strengths, talents, and skills function within the most critical areas of your life!

The good news is that all of this is possible. In fact, I dare say that it's the intention of your life. It's the answer to the top two questions humans ask and search for on Google: *Who am I?* and *What am I here for?* You should be able to articulate these answers. Could you imagine owning an incredibly expensive vehicle or home yet never knowing or getting to use its greatest features? That's you before entering into the discovery zone. Until you discover the strengths, talents, and skills that make you so special, you are the expensive luxury vehicle that just sits in the garage waiting to be discovered and put to use.

> **Discovery is about embracing the unknowns and gaining clarity regarding who you are before determining what you should do.**

This might sound simple, but there is far more substance here than you'd think. To get to this point in life requires a great deal of intentionality. I call this *digging*. In this chapter, we will do some digging that will lead you to discovering more of the greatness within you. The purpose of digging is to explore, which requires that we focus on the experience just as much as the results. In other words, enjoy this process! Discovery is about embracing the unknowns and gaining clarity regarding who you are before determining what you should do. This involves assessing your values, desires, and needs, while uncovering your strengths, gifts, talents, skills, personality, etc. I call this the *testing ground*.

The previous chapter involved only a few grains of the salt (value) you carry. In this chapter, I want to continue building by digging a little deeper. I am pleased to inform you that there's more; I'm also here to help you discover the more in your life! I will do so by referencing a parable to explain how to navigate the discovery process, share some important examples of how this zone has helped my life, and then challenge you to do some digging of your own. Let's begin!

PARABLE OF THE TALENTS

There once was a rich king who decided to be generous towards, and also test his three servants while he was away on a trip. To one servant, he gave five talents, to another two, and to the third servant, he gave one talent. Each were given according to their abilities. The servant who had received the five talents went and traded with his talents. Through trading, he was able to make another five talents. Likewise, the servant who had received two doubled his talents. However, the servant who had received one talent went and hid his talent in the ground. Eventually, the king of those servants came back from his travels and met up with them to settle all accounts.

The servant who had received five talents came and brought the talents saying, "King, you delivered to me five talents; look, I have gained five talents in addition to the ones you gave me."

The king said to him, "Excellent! You've proven yourself not only clever but loyal. You've executed a rather small task masterfully, so now I am going to put you in charge of something larger. But before you go back to work, come join my great feast and celebration."

Then, the servant who had been given two talents came forward, told the king how he'd turned his two talents into four, and then handed all four talents to the king. The king replied, "Excellent! You've proven yourself not only clever but loyal. You've executed a rather small task masterfully, so now I am going to put you in charge of something larger. But before you go back to work, come join my great feast and celebration."

Finally, the servant who had been given one talent came forward. He said to the king, "My lord, I know you are a hard man, difficult in every way. You make a healthy sum when others fail. You profit when other people are doing the work. You grow rich on the backs of others. Therefore, I was afraid, so I dug a hole and hid the talent in the ground. Here it is. You can have it back."

The king was furious! "You are a pathetic excuse for a servant! You have disproved my trust in you and squandered the generosity of talents I've given you. You know my talents always make a profit!

You could have at least put this talent into action to receive at least a little return or interest on it!"

Due to the third servant's lack of return, the king ordered his one talent be taken away and given to the servant who doubled his talents from five to ten.

Key points

1) You are a servant, and all the talents generously given to you are meant to be used in service.
2) Your talents have been entrusted to you with the expectation of a return.
3) You must know how all your talents and their value best serve. Otherwise, you will limit the effectiveness of these talents in your life and the lives of others, essentially burying them in the ground.

Let's address the greatest challenge we face in this zone. I call it the *lack attack* (cheesy, I know). A mentality of lack is an internal construct rooted in the seed of doubt. It's the state of believing you are without or do not have enough of something when, in all actuality, you live in abundance! The biggest trouble with the mentality of lack is this: whatever you focus on is what you will produce. This poor mental outlook is important to call out since doing so will help you gain awareness of the many disguises the mentality of lack can assume. Below, I have listed the 5 Lies of Lack we often fall prey to. Take careful note of each and assess whether or not one is currently allowed energy or residency in your mind.

Lack of Honor

There is a clear distinction between you and others. You are unique and highly valuable; there is no one like you. Yet no matter how many times I tell people this, there is a small voice inside us that seeks to contradict this truth. Many of us don't truly believe we are anything special; therefore, we don't value ourselves or our talents. The symptom of this belief is a lack of honor.

When we don't believe there is a generous amount of value given to us, we don't honor our talents or our lives as such.

When we don't believe there is a generous amount of value given to us, we don't honor our talents or our lives as such. Instead, we bury those talents under the pile of perceived insignificance we often develop. To bury our talents is to believe that our life is not meant for adding value to anyone else's, so why bother doing anything with our talents? The results of this belief are qualities such as a low self-image, self-centeredness, excessive laziness, poor judgment, disinterest in life and others, and most egregious, wasted time! If this is you, know that this is a normal internal conflict.

You are not some oddball. We all are presented with this challenge in some form or another.

The first step in overcoming this is understanding that honor takes place when we consider something or someone a rare opportunity. Your opportunity is to experience great pride, pleasure, and privilege in your talents. Imagine if you viewed your talents with this perspective. Take great pride in every person and thing you've been entrusted with, genuinely considering them to be a pleasure and a rare opportunity. It's a privilege to have the talents you've been given. Transforming this paradigm of lack will help you mature your perspective concerning the talents you've been given and the honor they deserve.

Lack of Trust

When we don't honor our talents, we reject our responsibility as trustees which squanders a tremedous amount of value. A trustee, by law, is a person given control or powers of administration over properties in trust, with a legal obligation to administer it solely for the purposes specified.

When we don't honor our talents, we reject our responsibility as trustees which squanders a tremendous amount of value.

Imagine with me for a moment that you designate me as trustee over a beautiful mansion. You have given me complete administration over it and instructed me to use it as a resource to serve other people. You've told me to invite in families, develop people with needs, yet also to enjoy it on other days when I can sit out by the pool, enjoy a pina colada, etc. Yet, picture this: One day, I decide to abandon my responsibility as trustee, leaving the home empty and without maintenance. The paint grows old, the lawn grows out of control, and eventually the home completely breaks down.

What would you say to me when you returned to see your property? How hurt would you be? How much of your trust would I have lost at this point? On a scale of one to ten, how willing would you be to kill me and hide the body if you knew you could get away with it? Think about what you feel and you will understand God's perspective when we prove to be untrustworthy trustees with the talents we've been given control and power of administration over. You carry an eternal obligation to do the necessary digging it will take to administer your talents solely for the purposes specified. Be someone who can be a worthy trustee.

Lack of Faith

A mentality of lack is also characterized by the absence of belief that your talents will profit. The king said to the servant, "You know my talents always make a profit!" I say the same to you. Your talents will ALWAYS make a profit. That's a promise, not an opinion. Don't allow this lack of faith mentality to convince you that there will not be a return on the talents you've been given. There is always a great return; in fact, there must be a return because that's why you and I are here! Don't stop digging until you begin to clearly understand and see a return in your life. The principle here is that there will be no lack found in the return of your talents, so have faith even if you're in a tough or uncertain season. I will discuss more on the topic of developing a return in all areas of your life in the next chapter.

In the meantime, I think it's worthwhile to assess some potentially tough questions here. What is it that causes you to doubt the talents within you, or doubt that those talents will profit your life and the lives of others? Really take a second to think about this. What beliefs are supporting this lie? They could be that life is too hard or that discovering and unpacking yourself is too difficult. Maybe you believe that, because of the actions of others, your talents can't make a profit. Finally, maybe its fear, your comfort zones, or feelings of inadequacy. Whatever the root cause is, I challenge you to break free from this mentality of lack. Have faith. The value of your life will always make a profit, but only if you allow.

Lack of Action

Finally, the king said to the servant, "You could've at least put this talent into action!" There's that seed again. How many of us have been robbed by inaction? I would suggest that we all have experienced this lack at some point in our life. Lack of action is characterized by the absence of effort, urgency, or awareness. I've seen this play out in my own life far too many times. "That requires too much work," has been my favorite quote at many points in my life. And while I must say there is something to be said about efficiency, working smarter not harder, the truth is that when it comes to your value and your talents, too much work should never be an acceptable response! Too much work to get a return on your life? To positively impact your family, friends, community, or world? Too much work to turn those service-based dreams into an incredible reality? There's never too much work for these types of outcomes!

I'm with you; the thought of when, what, where, and how you should put your talents into action can be overwhelming.

Now, I'm with you; the thought of when, what, where, and how you should put your talents into action can be overwhelming. However, it's important to keep in mind that just by taking the first step, you can unlock major returns. Do you remember when I said your talents will always make a profit? This is why taking action is so important. When you realize what's been placed within you has a guaranteed return, you are more prepared for the frustrating moments along the journey of action.

Notice something in the story we're using as reference. Whereas, everything was taken away from the servant who did nothing (took no action) with the talent he was given, the servant who did do something (took action) with his talents, received even more! There's a principle here. Taking action always produces something—even if that result isn't the intended one. Even if you fail miserably, that is still a great return. Yes, you read that correctly. Failure is a positive return. Why? Because you took action! We are taught in school that failure is an end result when it is actually an opportunity! An opportunity to learn.

You may have never been told this before, but I want to transform your paradigm of failure. There are few returns in life as valuable as learning and growth. Failure is nothing more than a tour guide in life. It is there to signal one of two things: either you've gone in the wrong direction, or you still need to grow before you can continue forward. This may sound like a silly example, but I remember playing video games as a kid like *Uncharted* or some other game that involved taking action in order to accomplish a goal or objective. There were levels that were pretty easy to navigate, but every now and then I would encounter a level requiring failure. I would have to endure the frustration of trying again, and again, and again, and again until finally breaking through to the next level. Each time I would have to ask myself, *Am I doing this wrong? Am I using the wrong approach or thinking?*

However, none of those reasons was the sole reason why I eventually figured it out. The main reason I figured it out is because I kept taking action and trying again and again. I need you to harness a similar determination in your life and your level of action. You can do this! I would dare to say you must do this. Why? Because the alternative is highly unpleasant. An experience I wouldn't wish on anyone. Let's reference the story again.

For the servant who made no profit but buried his talent in the ground, the king ordered that he be tied up and thrown outside into the utter darkness where there is miserable mourning and great fear. That sounds extreme, I know, but think back to the statement I made regarding those who experience a flavorless life. Their lives aren't much different from the miserable mourning description. When our lives lack action, our hands feel tied in uncertainty and frustration, ultimately leading to an utter darkness each day where there's no urgency for life. Sadly, we experience more dread, and on the worst days misery, each day becoming nothing more than a step closer to the end of existence. This should make us all mourn and be overcome with fear—not the unhealthy type of fear, but fear of missing out on discovering so much more in our lives due to inaction.

Hopefully, now you can see why the greatest challenge we face in this zone is possessing a mentality of lack. Don't fall prey to the lies. They will only harm you in the discovery zone of your life. Next, let's dive into the discovery formula.

THE DISCOVERY FORMULA

By now you realize that you carry eternal value. This value warrants a return. The talents in the story represent money; however, I wanted you to look at this story from the perspective of the talents representing the value within you. That way, we are all clear of what's at stake before moving on to the next section. The gifts, strengths, talents, skills, and overall value you've been given to share with the world is the stake. The key is discovering how to get a return on all that you've been given.

One would think the most important focus is the talent return. After all, it's what we've spent our time discussing during the opening of this chapter, but that's not the most important focus. More significant than what you get out of your life is who you become. This foundation determines the quality of your life's return.

Think of it this way: Picture a beautiful home, a home for you and your loved ones. Many of us determine the value and beauty of a home based on the home itself. The architecture, size, floor design, and other important features are all elements that cause our eyes to brighten and our hearts to race when we think about owning a beautiful home. As someone who loves going with the family to look at model homes for all these reasons, I will be the first to admit that they are very important. With that being said, though, I have seen enough homes to know that these elements aren't the most important value. The most important value of any home is the foundation it sits upon.

A wise man will build his house on a solid foundation. That way, when the rain comes pouring down, the streams begin to rise, and the winds beat against his house, it will be able to stand because it was built on a strong foundation. On the contrary, a foolish man will build his house on sand. When the rain comes down, the streams begin to rise, and the winds blow and beat against that house, it will fall with a great crash.

This is the image of what your life looks like if you're focused on gaining a return without first building a strong foundation of who you are. Clarity of who you are will serve great value when the inevitable rain, floods, and winds of life beat against your purpose, your value, and your return. No matter the amount of value, if our lives don't have a strong foundation, we will not be able to handle what we've been given.

> **No matter the amount of value, if our lives don't have a strong foundation, we will not be able to handle what we've been given.**

I'm willing to bet that the third servant did not desire this situation or intentionally pursue such a terrible outcome. I think it's safe to give this servant the benefit of the doubt. Imagine the servant's reaction when the king placed all this value in the lap of someone who most likely had never managed such great value before this point. Can you imagine the pressure he felt, the anxiety that might have consumed his heart each passing day of not gaining a return, knowing the king could come back any time? It's not a stretch to imagine that this servant was simply overwhelmed and stressed to the max, while trying to figure out how he would gain a return on these talents.

Many of us, if not all, have experienced this frustrating challenge. *How do I begin this discovery process? Where should I focus first? How do I know this is the right step? What if I lose everything? What if I'm not good enough, smart enough, qualified enough, educated enough, etc.?* As you can see, I could finish the remainder of this book by simply listing out all the stress-filled questions that often cause a paralysis of fear. Do these questions sound familiar to you? If so, your life is about to change! I'm about to share a formula that will help you establish a strong foundation, ensuring that challenging questions never cause you to bury your talents again!

Let's revisit the 5 Dream Types from earlier; however, this time we will use the five as a formula for digging into who you are. We will use each dream type as a prompt, helping you dig into the vital fundamentals of your life. This will provide a formulaic approach with the end goal of gaining a foundational clarity in your life. By following this formula, you will discover answers to questions such as how to create a vision for your life, where to focus first, what materials are at your disposal, and more. The hope is that this will help remove the pressure and ignite your passion for life. This will result in an increased confidence, leading to the greater return!

Exercise

The following is intended for discovery purposes only. Once again, limit judging your answers. Take the pressure off! I will repeat that again for greater emphasis: take the pressure off! Because you are in the assessment phase of these four zones (dreams, discovery, development, decisions), you will have plenty of time to execute and cut off the proverbial fat in the coming chapters. For now, simply think and record your answers as you work through these next exercises.

You may find these questions to be challenging. You may not be able to answer all of them, and that's perfectly fine. The goal here is action! The key is to keep coming back. Don't quit. The answers will reveal themselves the more you take action towards your destiny. Also, because I've learned over the years that not everyone thrives within conceptual thoughts, I've provided an overview of this section. Refer to it if you need to identify where you are within this overall concept. I hope this helps. Let's begin, shall we? (Be as specific as you can.)

Discovery Formula	Description
Fairy Tale	Establishing vision
Seasonal	Identifying sacrifice
Material	Life Builders: time and knowledge
Shared	Life Builders: network and money
Service	Unlocking your value offer

From Fairy Tale to Foundational Vision

Key point: A dream without the four elements of vision, goal, plan, and action is only a fairy tale. Begin adding some vision to your life by digging up your answers to the following questions. Take your time. Quick answers aren't nearly as valuable as thoughtful answers. You are worth the invested time. For questions 2-6, use the chart below, or visit thejoshuamentality.com and download the form.

1) What kind of life do you want?
2) What do you value most? (Write out your top 5-10 values.)

3) What are your top strengths, skills, and talents? (Examples: communicative, problem solver, decisive, creative, planning, strategy, input, detail-oriented, analytical, leader, etc.)
4) List your current roles and the future roles you wish to have. (Examples: father, community leader, teacher, songwriter/musician, lawyer, doctor, entrepreneur, professional, student, etc.)
5) Goal: Describe how you would like to add value in each role for those you serve? How do you want the people you care about and others to describe your contribution?
6) Ultimately, who must you become in each role to accomplish this goal?
7) What habits are you currently working on in order to become the person you aim to be?

Values 2.	Strengths 3.	Roles 4.	Goal 5.	Who Must You Become? 6.	Habits 7.

Exercise hack: *If you are having trouble answering the questions, this may be a good growth indicator. The good news is that there are plenty of resources that can help you discover answers to these questions. For instance, a quick Google search of "list of values" would provide a nice bank for you to read through and help determine the top 5-10 values that are most* *important to you. There are many assessments out there that can help you discover more about your strengths.* Clifton's StrengthsFinder is one I've found to be very helpful when discovering my strengths (more on this later). These are just a few examples to help you get started. Don't get stuck. The answers are already there; fall in love with the search!

Establishing a clear vision for your life will help you develop a consistent target and discover a reference point that will keep you on track towards defined success for your life. This was a major milestone for me, and if you've never conducted an exercise like this before, it will be a major milestone for your life also. Gaining clarity regarding your values, strengths, roles, who you would like to become, and who you are actually becoming, based on your current habits, is a major step in the discovery zone. We will expand on this in the next chapter as we focus on your development plan.

> **Establishing a clear vision for your life will help you develop a consistent target and discover a reference point that will keep you on track towards defined success for your life.**

Season of Sacrifice

Next in this formula is identifying sacrifice. The sacrifice might be your comfort zone, pride, old mentalities and beliefs passed down from family, circumstances, or environment. Whatever that sacrifice is you must identify it. Awareness gives way to growth. I grew up in the hood, so when I left home for college, I took the hood with me in several ways, one being how I dressed. I remember weighing all of a buck fifty soaking wet (That's 150 pounds for the non-Ebonics speakers.), yet walking around in size thirty-six jeans, XXL shirts, and a fitted cap with the sticker still on it because . . . ? I have no clue, but trust me. It was a thing!

Then, one day, I met a man named Victor. Now, Victor may not have been rich, but because I had not seen a home or cars as nice as his before that point in my life, to me, he was a millionaire! Victor took me under his wing, invited me into his home, let me watch sports in his huge home theater, and more. However, that wasn't what had the greatest impact on my life. Strangely enough, the most profound moment with Victor had nothing to do with his nice house, beautiful family, or lovable personality. It was a conversation in the middle of a McDonald's line that caused a massive paradigm shift, leading to the first of many small life changing sacrifices.

While standing in line, Victor turned to me and asked a question I will never forget. With his Spanish accent he said to me: "Bro, you have a nice strong physique. Why do you cover it up with such baggy clothes?" Victor knew I was a single guy at the time, so he probably thought he was just giving me some great dating advice or something. Furthermore, there's nothing technically wrong with wearing baggy clothes, but what really took place in that moment was that, for the first time, I actually thought about *why* I did something.

My beliefs, values, who I aspired to be, all bubbled up to the surface with that question. Not only had I not thought about why I dressed the way I dressed, but, as silly as it may sound, until that moment, I had never really considered why I did or believed anything. In fact, at that time I was so stubborn and prideful that I hadn't even given it a second thought. I'll take it a step further. I'm willing to bet that if I didn't know Victor, and he would've asked me that exact question, I almost surely would've responded with, "Because this is how I dress," followed up with a nice, "... you got a problem with that?" response.

The kind of sacrifice I'm referring to here is one that requires slaughtering old thoughts and surrendering possession of pride, stubbornness, harmful beliefs, and unhealthy comfort zones. That moment provided an opportunity to not just change my wardrobe but to completely tear down tarnished buildings (mentalities) in my mind, forfeiting that land back to its rightful Creator/Owner. You must be prepared to do the same.

You've most likely already begun this process with the previous foundational vision exercise. I would like to take that further. There are thoughts, beliefs, habits, actions, comfort zones, and outlooks you once held that the season has come for you to sacrifice. Lay them down to be analyzed, searched, surrendered, and—dare I say—slaughtered? We all have areas in our thinking, beliefs, and actions that we've never taken the time to ask, *Why do I do that? Why do I think that way, act that way, believe that lie?* I venture to say most of us stay in this position because it's just easier. It's less stressful to continue doing what we know and have done for an extended period of our lives.

The alternative is to break into the unknown where we will be faced with uncomfortable, challenging, maybe even life altering questions that will totally transform our mentality. As scary as that may sound, trust me when I tell you the pain and discomfort of making this shift is only seasonal. The sacrifice will be worth it in the end, so be encouraged. Exciting benefits will follow this season. Your growth will be exponential as you add further clarity to this new life. At this point, you will be better equipped to properly steward some very important resources.

Important reminder: While considering what you will sacrifice, remember the point about time horizons. We have to sacrifice in order to reach new levels of growth. This requires hard work; there's no way around it. Nothing valuable in life has ever been accomplished without a season of sacrifice. Even if you're not the one sacrificing, someone has to. I say this to draw your attention to the patience it will require. Sometimes we make a sacrifice in a day and don't see the reward until years later. That's why awareness of the time horizon is important. Understanding this principle will help your vision remain clear and sustain you through the growing pains that will inevitably occur.

MATERIALS FOR LIFE-BUILDING

If I wanted to build a strong home, I would need the best materials. Your life is no different. There are specific life-building materials that, when applied and understood, will help you build a strong life on the foundation and understanding you've established thus far. The greatest materials (also known as *currencies*) we have available to us are time, knowledge, network, and money.

> **The greatest materials (also known as currencies) we have available to us are time, knowledge, network, and money.**

Here's another analogy. If vision makes up the foundation of who you are in life, then these materials are the building blocks that further enhance the quality of your life. Once you establish an understanding of who you are, your values, strengths, goals, roles, and habits, focus your attention on adding the materials of time, knowledge, network, and money. The first step is to assess these four elements by analyzing your current materials. In other words, take a look at what you already have available to you. Many men and woman have built multimillion dollar businesses, ultra-fulfilling lifestyles, and accomplishments by simply understanding how to best leverage the resources already within their possession.

If you've ever felt like you don't have the right materials to greatly enhance the quality of your life, I'm here to help you rid yourself of the mentality of lack you've bought into. As we discussed already, this mentality will only slow you down or worse, prevent you from taking any action. With my past experience of buying into this lie, I realized one very important fact. More often than not, everything you have is everything you need. This means stop waiting on someone to show up with just the right materials, just the right resources in time, knowledge, network, and cash. Use what you have available to you, and figure the rest out as you grow. This is the best way to learn while you put in the required sweat equity to gain a return. Now that you understand what these materials are, let's get into how you can assess and grow these elements in your life.

Time

Assess your time usage. Count every second as significant because it is. Doing this will help you learn how to prioritize and gain awareness of what your current priorities truly are. Your heart will always be where your treasure is. In other words, your time is your greatest treasure and life-building material. The only way to know what you consider most important is by evaluating where you spend this treasure. Many people have bought into the lie that they don't have enough time to do the things they'd like to believe are most important. It's amazing how this lack of time mentality shifts when you actually take the time to assess where you are spending your time. Conduct this assessment, and you will realize that you had the desired time all along; you just weren't using it wisely. Gain awareness of where you're spending this precious treasure.

Priority Management

Focus is often defined as the center of interest. Therefore, the material of time is best utilized when we determine what to focus on, why that focus is important, and where that focus lands on the list of priorities. Prioritizing your life is the greatest return on the material of time. I had a wise friend once say that *we will reach success,* and when we look back, we will find that *much of our success had more to do with what we said "no" to versus "yes."* What does this mean? It means that, in today's world, there is an enormous number of distractions fighting for the one spot on our priority list. Taking the time to establish what our priorities are will help us avoid the danger of these distractions which lead to time (material) wasted.

I will give you a recommended priority list in the next chapter. For now, begin analyzing what your current priorities would be if you had to write down your top ten. Don't just read that line; actually do this. Write out what your priorities are currently; categorize them so you establish a baseline for the next chapter.

Time Management

Next, discover how you're spending your time by tracking your current productivity. Resources to conduct this assessment are a planner, timer (your phone should suffice), and an accountability partner (optional).

For the next week, record every hour of your day. This might sound like an annoying task, but TRUST ME. It will be worth it in the end. The goal is to uncover where you are spending your (material) time. Once you've completed this exercise for a week or two, review your results using the following questions:

- → Which tasks are taking up your time?
- → How much time are you wasting?
- → How does your time spent compare to your priority list?

It's important to collect *quantitative* data versus *qualitative* data (relying on what you feel or think—anecdotal data). Take this exercise seriously, and I guarantee that you will experience a breakthrough in your awareness. Lack of awareness is the greatest barrier to successful growth.

Underline this next point: no one maximizes their time 100 percent. Therefore, that is not the goal of this exercise. Again, the point here is to grow your awareness! If I can get you in the habit of knowing how you are spending the material of time, then the behavioral change process will gain a much quicker turn around, and you will be able to spot those seasons when you are slacking quicker and get yourself back on track without squandering large amounts of time. This ability to self-monitor and self-regulate will become a valuable growth accelerator to have in your arsenal.

Knowledge

The way a man thinks will determine who and what he becomes. The greatest contributor to the way we think is the knowledge we obtain. Many cute sayings and quotes emphasize the importance of knowledge in various aspects of our lives: "Leaders are readers," "Knowledge is power,"

"Lips that speak knowledge are a rare jewel," or my favorite which says, "A wise person is hungry for knowledge, while the fool feeds on trash." Regardless of which clever saying you choose, the fact is the same. Knowledge is one of the most accessible materials we can accumulate. The knowledge we store has a direct correlation to the lives we live, what we accomplish, and who we become. Knowledge grants us access to the greatest and most beneficial life principles.

Furthermore, a fun fact that many aren't aware of or have never considered is this. As humans, we were created with a phenomenal capability of storing massive amounts of data and knowledge. Excuse me for a second as I geek out. Check out these facts highlighted by Suzanne Wu quoting *Science Express*[1]:

- → "Looking at both digital memory and analog devices, the researchers calculate that humankind is able to store at least 295 exabytes of information. (Yes, that's a number with twenty zeroes in it.) Put another way, if a single star is a bit of information, that's a galaxy of information for every person in the world. That's 315 times the number of grains of sand in the world. But it's still less than one percent of the information that is stored in all the DNA molecules of a human being."
- → "In 2007, humankind successfully sent 1.9 zettabytes of information through broadcast technology such as televisions and GPS. That's equivalent to every person in the world reading 174 newspapers every day."
- → "On two-way communications technology, such as cell phones, humankind shared 65 exabytes of information through

---

[1] Suzanne Wu, "How Much Information Is There in the World?" *ScienceDaily*, 11 Feb. 2011, https://www.sciencedaily.com/releases/2011/02/110210141219.htm.

telecommunications in 2007, the equivalent of every person in the world communicating the contents of six newspapers every day."

Many of us aren't aware of the amount of knowledge we have access to regarding who we are and how we best serve on this earth.

Here's where the dilemma lies. Many of us aren't aware of the amount of knowledge we have access to regarding who we are and how we best serve on this earth. After reviewing the facts above, it's safe to say that we are capable of storing and retrieving an enormous amount of knowledge. Yet, I've seen the potential of too many lives perish due to a lack of knowledge.

How is that possible with so much knowledge available to us today? The knowledge we store has a direct correlation to the lives we live, what we accomplish, and who we become. When you consider our extraordinary capacity, one would think with all the free access we have to knowledge capable of transforming our lives, that we would all be living purpose-filled, successful lives. Why is that not the case? Well, having access to a world of knowledge and knowing which knowledge is most beneficial to access are two totally different things. You have an abundance when it comes to capacity, access, and knowledge material. The missing key is stewardship.

Strength, Talents, and Skills

Do you know what your top strengths, talents, and skills are? We touched on this point in the section on establishing a vision for your life, but now I'd like to spend a little more time emphasizing the importance here. Growing up, I realized I had a talent for music. My grandmother described me as a baby crawling around on the floor with shoe boxes as my first preferred percussion instrument. That later grew into my first drum set. After years of playing drums in my local church, I began to hear melodies in my head which led me to pick up a cheap plastic Casio piano and teach myself how to play keys. From there I began writing, singing, and then speaking. These evolved into pursuing a degree in Interpersonal and Organizational Communication, finally obtaining my masters in Organizational Psychology.

Do you see how discovering your strengths, talents, and skills can lead to so much more? I discovered these things without any specific formula or idea of what I was doing at the time. Looking back and studying those years of my life and the lives of others have helped me discover and develop the formula I am walking you through now. Everything I described in my story came from a kid who had ZERO clue what he wanted to do his senior year in high school. The only things I knew for sure were that I possessed a talent, and I loved impacting people. So, my point is don't feel bad if you don't have everything figured out yet. That's what this section is all about—getting you started with your proverbial shovel in hand, digging through some of the hints and signs that point us all in the direction we should go.

As you have probably figured out, I never became a world-renown musician, singer, producer, etc. However, the knowledge of my talents, strengths, and skills granted me a sense of direction in life. My ability to write music enhanced a skill that allowed me to write this book. My ability to sing in front of audiences enhanced my ability to stand and speak in front of audiences. These are just two small examples of why it's important to dig into your talents, strengths, and skills. You never know where they may lead you.

Like me, your life may not unravel the way you think it will. Life doesn't end there, though. There's still greatness within and for you. And for the person saying, "But Joshua, I don't have any talents, strengths, or skills," that is a lie. Don't you accept this false insignificance for one more day! Tear that mentality down to the ground! You carry strengths, gifts, talents, and skills. You just haven't done enough digging yet. Dig by accessing available knowledge that will help you discover more.

Here's your starting point. For the next two weeks, check out the list below and designate some time to take a few or all of the following assessments. This will further add clarity to your knowledge of who you are and how you best serve. In addition, this will provide direction for where to focus your development efforts as you will not only discover your strengths, talents, and skills, but you will also discover a baseline for each that will come in handy during the development section.

Helpful Assessments		
Skills	Strengths	Leadership
The Self-Directed Search	Cliftons Strength Finders	DISC Behavioral
Big Five Personality Test	VIA Character Strengths Survey	'Who Am I?' Test
110Success.io	110Success.io	110Success.io

This is by no means a comprehensive list of assessments and resources. If an assessment you've taken is not on this list, that doesn't mean it's not a good one. I may have simply not taken it yet. Generally, speaking, I recommend you take as many assessments concerning your skills, strengths, talents, etc., as possible. However, do so with the goal of assessing trends. If every assessment is giving you entirely different trends in relation to your skills, strengths, and talents, then I encourage you to speak with a coach who can help you sort through the clutter and confusion. You can access these types of resources by visiting 110Success.io.

Bonus

This is an extra nugget to further transform the way you think about knowledge. This alone can change your life if you get it. Knowledge is a form of wisdom. There are two levels of wisdom in life: applied knowledge and applied belief. The first, applied knowledge, is acquired anytime you put knowledge into practice. That is wisdom because you were wise enough to know, *If I apply this knowledge, I will get a positive result.* The second level is what I like to call *sacred wisdom.* Sacred wisdom is *applied belief*! This wisdom comes from someone greater than you.

Sacred wisdom is God-breathed wisdom. This is the highest level of wisdom. And here's the phenomenal thing about this level of wisdom. Are you ready for this? This is about to blow your mind because you will never again have an excuse to not have content ideas, know what decision to make, or know when to make a decision. Sacred wisdom is available upon request! Free! Readily available. All you have to do is ask for it!

Could you imagine if I told you, "Hey, you want a million dollars? Okay, all you have to do is ask." How quick from the time my mouth finished that sentence, would you be asking for your million? The Bible tells us that God gives wisdom freely to those who seek and search for her like lost treasure. Those who seek understanding treat sacred wisdom like fine gold or silver. God gives it freely, freely! God-breathed wisdom for free! You don't have to sign up for subscription, pay a cover charge, execute a series of tasks. You don't have to do anything but exchange the number one currency in the world, which is time. You have to make the time to pick up the free wisdom. You have to make the time to fine-tune the connection so that you may hear and receive the wisdom from God's mouth to your being. Sacred wisdom is one of the greatest gifts on earth.

SHARED LIFE-BUILDING MATERIALS
Networks

You need a network, a team, or a *village*, as I like to call it. A group of people to share the great return of your life's value. It's been said that your *network* will determine your *net worth*. As played out as this statement may seem, it is truth! Walk with the wise, and you will become wise. Walk with the rich, and you will become rich (internally and externally). However, walk with fools, and you will suffer great harm to your purpose and destiny.

Now is a great time to audit your network! I believe one's network is the cheat code in life. The easy button, the difference between a car with automatic windows and the old manual roll-me-down. The roll-me-down represents when we go through life trying to figure everything out on our own instead of engaging a healthy community where we can learn from and grow with others. If you've followed my work long enough, you've heard me exhaust this point. It's worth doing again, though.

First I must point out that I am not referring to networking here. That term and practice has been diminished and contaminated in many ways due to ineffective and self-centered business practices. I'm referring to relationships. A great network should consist of authentic, service-centered relationships. The opposite of this is transactional, self-seeking relationships. A great network creates group synergy around a shared goal which yields exceptional results in every area of life. A network can supplement your weaknesses.

Using the previous assessments, you determined what your strengths and weaknesses are. It's time for you to supplement those weak areas by building your team. Refer back to the previous chart you completed where you listed your strengths. What are the opposites of your strengths? What areas do you have to work at to do well, and even then, you only graze the surface of proficiency? Administrative skills, planning, strategy, marketing, sales, etc.? The key is to consider what you don't do well, so you can begin to think about what networks may be best suited for you.

The best way to confirm whether or not you have a great network is by measuring the impact of that network on your life. How are the people making you better, challenging you, uplifting you, inspiring you to serve? These are all great questions and indicators for joining or leaving a network. If you are trying to go through life all by your lonesome, you are taking the long route! If you want to accomplish or capture anything large in your life, your chances increase exponentially when you serve within a network.

Below, I've listed four more attributes of a healthy and beneficial network. You can use this as a guide to measure your current network, build your own network, and upgrade or completely shift into a healthier network. A great network provides many things.

Strength

Your network should provide strength. A triple-braided cord is not easily broken. It is easier to break an individual than it is to break an entire group. There is strength in numbers. One way to know if a principle is true or not is by inverting it. Strength in numbers is true both in the positive sense and the negative. As Stephen Covey says, "The noise of urgency creates an illusion of importance."[2] As we look across society, we can see examples of strength from groups whose intentions aren't good, yet they seem to gain influence at times. Why? Because they have the ability to develop a network of people who, together, increase the noise around subjects in order to drive up the sense of urgency. This is the principle of strength in numbers at work. Even in a negative context, the principle remains true. How much more valuable, then, could this principle be for your life? The answer is extremely valuable.

If you've ever struggled, or find yourself currently struggling with creating a sense of urgency in your life, discovering your network can provide a tremendous boost. Think about the benefits of igniting urgency within those important, yet dormant, areas of your life that lack energy. Simply having a strong network could be the push you need to unleash new levels of urgency in your life, catapulting you towards every accomplishment you desire to achieve. If you sincerely want to experience the benefits of a strong network that will help you accelerate your growth, check out the 110Success community at 110Success.io.

Support

If one person falls, another can reach out and help, but someone who falls alone is in real trouble. Have you ever felt alone in life? Like no one cares if you disappeared or fell on hard times? Your network should provide

---

[2] "The Noise of Urgency Creates an Illusion of Importance," *QuoteTab*, https://www.quotetab.com/quote/by-stephen-r-covey/the-noise-of-urgency-creates-an-illusion-of-importance?source=noise.

support and accountability. The support of having a network that will reach out and help you in those times of need is invaluable. Many enter into deep depression, low mental health, or worse—suicidal thoughts and actions—simply because there was no one there to pull them from their lonely slumber.

"I don't need anyone else," is something we often hear said in our society; however, this pride-fueled statement couldn't be further from the truth. We are made better by others. You could walk this life alone and accomplish great things by yourself, but it wouldn't be nearly as fulfilling as enjoying it with others. There's a description of this sentiment found in the book of Ecclesiastes. It describes a man who is all alone, without a child or a brother, yet who works hard to gain as much wealth as he can. But then he reflects to himself, *Who am I working for? Why am I giving up so much pleasure now? It is all so meaningless and depressing.*

This is a sad yet common description of many hard-working solo or siloed men and women. Don't go through life thinking the goal is to work hard in order to gain wealth just so you can enjoy it by yourself. This is a trap that will lead to a meaningless and depressing life. Your network is your support system. Identify who these people are, and allow them to support you and your work with love, joy, constructive and encouraging feedback, prayer, valuable resources, and more. You will be so happy you allowed yourself to receive this benefit of having a network.

Safety

A person standing alone can be attacked and defeated, but two can stand back-to-back and conquer. A network should provide safety. Sometimes the greatest protection we need is from ourselves. Having a network of service-centered authentic relationships can provide timely wisdom when major decisions come up in your life and guidance when you're unsure of how to execute a particular task, project, or position. Your network of service-centered, authentic relationships also provides a safe place to fail.

Over the years I've made some pretty immature decisions and taken actions that in the moment seemed correct. I was sure I needed to take that stance, respond that way, or preserve that unhealthy mentality. I'm thankful the people in my network didn't crush me. Instead, they protected me; they stood back-to-back covering me while I worked through some major growing pains. Do you have a network like this? If not, you should strongly consider finding or creating one yourself.

One of the most profound examples of a person I can think of who demonstrates the value of this network attribute is a mentor of mine named Pastor Mike Gonzalez. He played a key role in preserving my current family before I even realized I wanted a family. There was a time when I thought marriage was a limiting idea. I was blessed to know Mike who achieved building an admirable, loving, and honorable marriage. Can you believe I would sit with this guy badgering him with questions about why he would ever want to settle down with one woman? I remember how he would patiently and lovingly smile while listening to my nonsense, then simply share the beauty of what he and his wife had developed. It left an impression on me.

I didn't realize it then, but he was providing a safe space for me to be honest, transparent, and protected and shed the immature beliefs I held. Those moments had a direct impact on the husband and father I am today. You can experience the same. Having a safe place to grow and fail is crucial to our development. Pay close attention to this attribute when joining or creating your own network. It's the network attribute that's most often overlooked and underestimated as people focus more on glorifying results over growth and journey.

Strategy

Two people are better off than one, for they can help each other succeed. As a strategist, I've witnessed the exhilarating clarity that accompanies a great plan. I've worked with clients who came to me feeling stuck or low in spirit and confidence, and with one good strategic idea, their entire outlook, expectations, and confidence sky rocketed. We all need this at times. A network provides this kind of uplift, encouragement, and so much more! This may sound extreme, but bear with me. There's a million-dollar strategy, idea, or partnership waiting for you within a healthy network. Eternal value will enhance your life in ways that you never imagined, granting you a sense of identity, purpose, and fulfillment—all found within a healthy, values-centered network. This proverbial life-building material has been my saving grace during many seasons.

There was once a time in my professional career when, to be completely honest, I really sucked at being a professional. Although I had a desire to own a business one day, I had no clue what actually went into leading a business. Sure, I could talk a good game, but when it came down to it, I was as green as they came in business and professionalism. It wasn't for lack of desire but rather, I simply wasn't exposed to a network of established high-caliber business men and women. Most of my success until that point could be attributed to instincts, a willingness to serve, and a love for people. (Those values will get you far; that's another book for another day, though).

In order to change this, I had to find a network that would help me discover more about myself, my strengths, talents, and skills. In addition, it needed to demonstrate how great leadership should look, feel, and serve. I instinctively knew this would help me grow into the leader required to accomplish all the desires in my heart. So, I set out to find work after graduating from UCF (the University of Central Florida) with two parameters in mind. I wanted to work for a company that had a mission I could get excited about every day, and I wanted a leader and team that would help me grow. I found that in one of the most unexpected places.

I ended up spending seven years working at AdventHealth—yes, healthcare of all places (never saw that coming)—under one of the greatest leaders I've had the pleasure of serving—Zorayma Barnard. This network is where I discovered and developed the strategy for my career and future. Think about that! Understand the difference in perspective here. Seeing my job as a network, not a prison sentence, allowed me to leverage it towards discovery, growth, and tons of fun! When I chose AdventHealth as my place of service, the most important qualities to me were mission and leadership. I could take less money, but the nonnegotiables were those two elements. That was a strategic move with network at the forefront of my mind. Why? Because during my discovery stage I realized that I possessed strong leadership attributes that needed further development. Knowing that leadership is DNA (the leader you serve under is often the leader you become), strategically drove me towards a great network.

Seeing my job as a network, not a prison sentence, allowed me to leverage it towards discovery, growth, and tons of fun!

You know there's a question coming. The question is this: how can your current network(s) serve your strategy? Think about all the groups you are a part of currently, and consider how these networks are adding clarity to your life and future either from a career standpoint or as a leader. What areas are you weak or underdeveloped in, and how will your network strategically help you grow? Who can you partner with or serve under to sharpen your skills and enhance your knowledge, mentality, professionalism, and business acumen?

Don't move forward until you have seriously taken time to think about these things. This is vital life-building material. Two people are better off than one, for they can help each other succeed. Identify which network(s) will provide you with the strength, support, safety, and strategy you need for success.

Money

This is the life-builder that comes to mind first when many of us think about building a great life. Contrary to common practice and belief, money is actually the least important life-building material on this list. Just in case you missed that, *money is not the most important life-building material.* It's last because it is not as valuable as the other three. Money is a tool that should be used to build or acquire things that serve people. That's why you will notice that money is listed under the shared section of materials. The mere concept of money is purposed for transactions or exchanges in order to obtain value. It's not a representation of one's value—huge difference!

Growing up in the hood I use to think that money could solve all my problems. If I could just make a million dollars, my problems would evaporate into the sky, and I'd be able to spend the rest of my life comfortably. That was a foolish thought, and after finally making some money, I realized those problems did not evaporate into thin air. In fact, they only exposed more problems . . . including the quality of my character. Now, I say that in order to establish a fundamental principle: money is not the most important thing. Once you have a high understanding of who you are and how you best serve, money will find you, and lots of it. Now that we've established this truth, I can, in good conscience, encourage you to make and build as much money as you can. Money in the hands of people who understand that money is meant to build and acquire things that serve people is a game changer. These people transform lives and communities.

I introduced you to the top three life-building materials first because, if you can capture the eternal value of those three, you will use your money to acquire more time, knowledge, and network, which will grow an ecosystem of wealth around you, leading to a life that is extremely fulfilling. I'll share a money secret with you that I learned early on that caused a seismic shift in my finances. Are you ready? Here it is:

Time + Knowledge + Network = Lots of money!

That's it. It's not more complex than that.

I've watched people chase money with a strong passion only to be left drained, slaving away for the paper, empty from getting the paper and it not resulting in the fulfillment they thought it would, or just flat out broke from failing to achieve the financial success they desired. Contrast this with someone who uses the secret I shared with you by taking the time to search and prioritize their dreams, dig within themselves in order to obtain the knowledge of who they are and how they best serve (fundamental life vision, strengths, talents, and skills), and finally, accelerate their results by joining a group of liked-minded people. This person would become a money magnet! Why? Because this person would clearly understand and be able to articulate their value. When you understand your value, you can monetize that value at a greater level.

Compare this with the plague of a meaningless desperation for money. Willing to do and trade anything for a material that would come to you with ease if you focused all your attention on the top three materials. Money is a byproduct of time, knowledge, and network, not the other way around. We seek money to have more freedom of our time, access to knowledge, and membership in prestigious networks. Therefore, I encourage you to use your money to do the same, even if you don't have lots of it as you read this. I believe and have experienced that when people shift their attention to the advice here, they achieve an increase of life-building material in the form of money.

There's so much more on this topic that I could spend an entire book covering it. The purpose of this section, though, is to upgrade your mentality. Therefore, focus on these fundamental points. What's your mentality around money and its importance based on your life actions and habits? Have you sacrificed maximizing time, knowledge, and network in a pursuit for more money? If so, it's never too late to correct this misalignment. Get back on track and focus on leveraging the more important life-building materials, and the money will have no choice but to be attracted towards you!

Have you sacrificed maximizing time, knowledge, and network in a pursuit for more money?

SERVICE

Now that you've made it this far through the discovery formula, you should possess a greater understanding of your makeup and the value within you and at your disposal. The value you've dug up while working through this formula is meant to serve the world; therefore, the final step in this formula is determining how you best serve. The best way to do this is by putting into practice what you've discovered about yourself thus far (go out and serve). By doing so, you will discover how you best serve.

Serving enhances clarity of direction in our lives. To see the power of serving demonstrated, let's refer to the story I told at the beginning of this section: The Parable of the Talents. The difference between the first two servants and the last servant was their willingness to get out and serve. In other words, they put their talents to work! The only way you can gain a return on all you've discovered thus far, is by putting these things into practice. Now is a great time to review all that you've discovered. Look back on the work you've accomplished in this section, and take time to envision how all the value you've dug up translates into your life.

As a little boy, I often envisioned myself carrying an imaginary yellow Batman utility belt around with me everywhere I went. This belt had the power to do anything I wanted: freeze time, go forward and backwards into the future, convince the girl in my elementary class to like me—you know, cover all my bases. While that utility belt was only a product of my wild imagination, what you've dug up in this chapter is a real-life utility belt. You now have more than enough information and insight into yourself, to begin putting your very own utility belt together and carve out how you best serve.

Let's recap the elements that you now have at your disposal.

1) We covered the top challenges you must continue to avoid as you serve with what you've discovered. Go back and review the mentalities of lack if you need a refresher.
2) We then worked through the discovery formula, where you put in the time establishing your vision, gaining a baseline of your goals, values, strengths, and habits. From there, we assessed where sacrifice may be warranted, old mentalities you will have to surrender or destroy to prepare the ground of your life for digging.
3) Next, we introduced the life builders of time, knowledge, network, and money. I hope that you will make these your new best friends, leveraging their benefits to produce great fruit in your life.
4) Finally, we've made it to the last step in this formula—service—which is how you gain a return on the value you've dug up in this section.

Your next step is to begin incorporating what you've learned into your daily practices while also seeking out new spaces to experiment and test. If you are still unsure of how or where to put into practice what you've discovered, here's a good start. Find a community that will allow you to test out all the value you've discovered. This could be a job or an organization that provides community service opportunities, etc. If you discovered that you are a good speaker or have a strong skill in strategy for instance, look for spaces where you can serve with these talents.

Remember that serving enhances clarity of direction. Don't let all you've found go to waste. Put these things into practice; trade them in and out of the marketplace. Pay attention to what you like—what inspires you, fulfills you, or drains you. These are indicators that you want to capture, so you know what areas you need to invest in developing even more. This will set you up nicely for the next chapter and help you achieve the goal of spending the rest of your life doing what fulfills you and allows you to best serve.

Pay attention to what you like— what inspires you, fulfills you, or drains you. These are indicators that you want to capture, so you know what areas you need to invest in developing even more.

Most of the work you've done thus far has focused around discovering your value. From here, we will transition into how you can *develop* the value you've discovered and shift from assessment (search + digging), to execution (growth + legacy). You have a better understanding of who you are (dreams, strengths, talents, skills, etc.), and how your value best serves. I want to congratulate you if you've made it to this point. That means you've endured some very hard work. You've asked and answered some very challenging questions that have caused you to dig deeper into you.

Further solidify this work by reviewing the reflection questions before moving on to the next chapter. Once again, I'm going to press on you here. Do not skip this portion. These reflection questions are important and intentionally positioned to help you fully absorb the value you've dug up. The psychology behind these questions is calculated. They are not a space filler, so do them! Okay, I'm done insisting now. See you in the development zone!

REFLECTION

1) What is your greatest takeaway from this chapter?

2) We covered quite a lot in this chapter. Which points should you go back and review?

3) What were the most challenging moments or points in this chapter and why?

4) Now that you've completed the discovery formula, what was the most important thing you discovered about yourself?

5) How will this chapter impact your life moving forward?

6) Find someone to share what you've discovered. Who will that person be, and when will you be sharing with them?

CHAPTER 3

DEVELOPMENT

LEVERAGE YOUR VALUE FOR GOOD IN EVERY AREA OF YOUR LIFE!

Once upon a time there was a very strong woodcutter. He asked a timber merchant for a job, and he got it. The pay was very good; so were the work conditions. And for those reasons the woodcutter was determined to do his very best. His boss gave him an axe and showed him the area in the forest where he was to work.

The first day, the woodcutter cut down eighteen trees.

His boss was impressed and said, "Well done. Keep it up. You are our best woodcutter yet." Motivated by his boss's words, the woodcutter tried even harder the next day, but he only cut down fifteen trees. The third day he tried even harder, but only cut down ten trees.

Day after day the woodcutter cut down fewer and fewer trees. His boss came to him and told him that if he did not chop down more trees each day, he would lose his job. The woodcutter needed the job, so he tried harder and harder. He worked during his lunch breaks and tea breaks, but still he could not cut down enough trees. *I must be losing my strength*, the woodcutter thought to himself. He worked overtime, but still, it was not enough.

Eventually his boss came to him and told him he was fired. The woodcutter was really upset, but he knew that he had worked as hard as he could and just did not have enough time to chop more trees. He sadly handed his axe back.

The boss took one look at the axe and asked, "When was the last time you sharpened your axe?"

"Sharpen my axe?" the woodcutter replied. "I have never sharpened my axe. I have been too busy trying to cut down enough trees."

When was the last time you sharpened your axe?

There are great words of wisdom in Ecclesiastes 10:10. They serve as a reminder that if your axe is dull and you don't sharpen its edge, then you will exert more strength. That's because wisdom is the advantage that brings success. Having a development plan for your life is wisdom. A development plan helps you maintain a focused life and keeps your value sharpened, ensuring that you are prepared to chop down those gigantic goals you may have, providing vision that cuts through the fog of uncertainty in your life, and growing your strength and capacity as a leader.

> **If your axe is dull and you don't sharpen its edge, then you will exert more strength.**

Development is an everyday thing. Every day we take one small or major step forward or backwards. Every day, no exceptions! Like the woodcutter, if you aren't paying close attention, it can be difficult to tell if your axe is getting sharper or duller. Many of us have bought into the false belief that working harder is the key to success. That if we somehow just get up every day to work twenty, forty, sixty hours or more a week and chop down as many trees as we can, we will reach success. This couldn't be further from the truth.

Many of you work extremely hard. Each day you swing that axe with all your strength, trying harder and harder to keep up with the demands, sacrificing pleasures and enjoyment, in order to dedicate more energy towards reaching success. Yet, despite all that effort, it still isn't enough! If this sounds familiar, you are the woodcutter. As I shared with you in previous chapters, time is your greatest currency. Therefore, it is crucial that you spend it wisely. Chopping down the trees of your life with a dull axe is unhealthy, unpleasant, and unwise. This is why you need a development plan for your life. You have to not only know how to sharpen your axe, but have a plan for when and where to focus your attention to sharpening. This chapter will help you develop just that.

Here we will combine your work from the previous two chapters. They focused on assessment, searching your dreams, and digging up, assessing, analyzing, and discovering all the great value within you. By now, you should have a really great understanding of how awesome you are! This chapter will focus on how you can leverage your value by developing a plan for your life (execution).

Some would say there's no way to plan for life due to all the unpredictable twists and turns that it often brings. There is some truth to that statement; however, it can be misleading. While you cannot literally predict what will happen two years from now, you can have a plan for what your priorities will be, how you will measure your capacity, and how you will manage your time. The assessment portion of this book was designed to help produce clarity in your life regarding who you are. Development is about focusing that clarity into a structured plan, leading to high value production in every area of your life. This is called *high-capacity leadership*.

High-capacity leadership centers around two developmental pillars: value development and priority development. Before we focus on these pillars, though, I'd like to take a moment to establish a foundation for the mentality required in order for this chapter to be effective in your life. Let's unpack the significance of focusing on process which is the fundamental driver of your development plan.

PROCESS > OUTCOMES

Focusing on your development helps to reformat your mind, centering your measurement efforts around what really matters. It's the difference of measuring your life by the more effective metrics of process and prioritization versus the short-sighted mentality that measures outcomes and results. While outcomes and results do have their importance, greater value and sustaining power derives from focusing on continual development, recognizing that success is a continuous motion of growth, not a destination.

Let's further discuss this paradigm shift of process over outcomes. Many of us have been told that results are all that matter and have been rewarded based on this criterion. I want to challenge this idea. Let's look back at the woodcutter story for a moment. Notice the response from the woodcutter's boss when he cut down the first eighteen trees. He was very impressed with the outcome and held the woodcutter in high regard for that day, labeling him the "best woodcutter yet!" After hearing these words, the woodcutter was super motivated and focused solely on outcomes from that moment on, forgetting that the higher value was his process. This is a lesson in leadership and process development, but for our purposes I will focus on the process portion.

We have all made this mistake before. Striving for the approval of others regarding our outcomes, connecting our self-value perception or intrinsic motivation to the outcome or results. Outcome-based development leads to poor measurement systems, where we often despise small beginnings and small progress due to lesser outcomes than expected or previously experienced. Outcome-based development leads to unnecessary pressure, an unbalanced life, emotional and irrational decisions, extreme fatigue, poor self-image and self-talk, and an acceptance of self-limiting beliefs! Yes! All of this from simply over focusing on outcomes instead of process.

Outcome-based development leads to unnecessary pressure, an unbalanced life, emotional and irrational decisions, extreme fatigue, poor self-image and self-talk, and an acceptance of self-limiting beliefs!

Process is about focusing on micro learnings, translated into macro actions (referring to the quality of your actions not the quantity), which produce massive results! Here's an example. Let's say you have been experiencing high levels of stress lately, causing a strain on your mental health. You decide to do something about this by focusing on improving your overall mental health. The improvement would be the outcome, your process would involve finding a small starting point.

Let's say you realize all the clutter in your home is one of the main contributing factors to your stress level increase, but you've noticed this before, and you just can't seem to keep the clutter out. This spins you into a cycle of frustration. This is the perfect example of an outcome-centered approach. The key here would be shifting your efforts to a process-centered approach. Instead of conducting your usual cleaning and decluttering spree, which requires a great deal of energy that's difficult to sustain, imagine if you broke this change into a process. Maybe instead of decluttering the entire space, you could concentrate on a small area for a few weeks until that becomes a habit.

If you focus on fixing your bed, growing this habit would increase your overall morale towards the outcome goal of mental health improvement. It's also easier to sustain overtime. Once you have the bed-fixing process down, you could then expand to that corner of clothes that seems to always pile up on the chair (or if you're me, in the bathroom). See how this approach accomplishes the same outcome as your clean-everything-in-one-day outcome-based approach? Focusing on process will create long-term sustainability and expansion which will lead to greater results!

This paradigm shift of process over outcomes applied to your overall life will be critical in your development journey. Focusing on process takes the pressure off, removing the desperate striving for outcomes that don't last very long due to the lack of sustainability that only processes can create. This outlook shifts your focus towards a more strategic, purpose-filled plan for life.

Falling in Love with Process

Now that I've convinced you of the importance of focusing on processes more than outcomes, I must warn you that the reason many don't focus on process is because it isn't as glamorous and immediately gratifying as outcomes. The greatest example of this can be found in an article written by Micah Cartee[3] where he talks about the process of the Chinese Bamboo Tree.

This tree begins as a nut planted in soil and must be watered and fertilized every single day for five years before it finally breaks through the ground.

All that time, it spreads out its roots, and if at any time the watering or fertilizing process stops, the Chinese Bamboo Tree dies in the ground. However, in that fifth year, the Chinese Bamboo Tree finally breaks through the ground and grows to nearly ninety feet tall in just six weeks! The tree must take five long years of developing a strong, deep, wide root system so it doesn't topple over when it is grown.

Think about that for a second, five years of consistent, everyday watering or you lose everything. Thank God our development isn't as stringent.

---

3 Micah Cartee, "Trust the Process – God's Plan for Fulfilling His Promises for Your Life," *JRC*, 31 May 2018, https://jamesriver.church/blog/trust-the-process.

There are similarities between the Chinese Bamboo Tree and us, though. If you want to experience the outcome and benefits of having a development plan for your life like becoming a high-capacity leader, then you must make a decision to fall in love with the process. Cherish it, tie it around your neck, write it on all of the windows of your heart and soul! Process! That's the commitment required to gain the greatest return from this chapter.

> **Love the process! Embrace all the internal work, hidden out of sight from the world yet taking place within you as you develop the strong, deep, wide root systems.**

Before we cover any concept or additional point, I need your undivided commitment: Love the process! Embrace all the internal work, hidden out of sight from the world yet taking place within you as you develop the strong, deep, wide root systems that will help you grow into the leader required to add high value in every area of your life. Focus on watering your life daily with the principles we are about to explore. If you do this, you will develop your life in a way that is more satisfying than any outcome you could ever imagine! And that is not an exaggeration.

BECOMING A HIGH-CAPACITY LEADER

Development and scale are two words that brighten any business owner's heart. Your business grows and you get to experience great returns and growth at every level. Why? Because you've developed your systems to the point where your business can now successfully develop and scale. In essence, the development and scalability of a business are determined by its systems. In more simplistic terms, systems ensure that your business is prepared for growth and responsibility. The concept of high-capacity leadership is no different.

> **High-capacity leadership systems center around those two developmental pillars--value development and priority development.**

High-capacity leadership focuses on value development, scale, and distribution. In order to execute this approach, we must develop systems in our life that equip us for large growth and responsibility. This bears repeating: the key here is the systems. High-capacity leadership systems center around those two developmental pillars—value development and priority development—that we will now explore.

The following attributes are often demonstrated by high-capacity leaders:
- → Generate large amounts of value.
- → Distribute high value consistently across multiple areas.
- → Exhibit discipline in their systems focus.
- → Develop influence across several industries and interests.
- → Clearly sense their priorities.

- → Can be trusted with large amounts of responsibility.
- → Know when and where to channel their energy.
- → Produce a successful and attractive life.

High-Capacity Leaders Develop Their Value.
Continuous growth and value readiness are the markings of a high-capacity leader. The goal is to consistently look for ways to grow yourself so that you are always ready to distribute value. This form of leadership is a universal currency. The world can never have too many great value-based leaders. Leadership is applicable and highly valued in any family, community, industry, or business. Think about that for a second. For this reason, over the past decade, leadership development has become a hot topic at the business and personal level.

Many leadership styles and competencies have surfaced over the years, creating a wonderful ecosystem of leadership lessons, principles, teachings, concepts, and practices. Having such a vast, diverse set of leadership tools and resources is great; however, high-capacity leadership development is distinct versus the universal leadership development approach many of us have experienced. High-capacity leadership development concentrates on developing your value, centering around assessing your specific strengths, skills, and talents, then building a comprehensive and process-centered development plan around it. This approach is in contrast to a more universal leadership development approach. This is important to point out.

Over the years, far too often people have approached leadership development without a targeted plan. While the *benefits* of leadership development are universal, your *approach* to leadership development should not be. Here's what I mean. The best leadership development plan for your life is one that is customized to your life, your value! Leadership is influence. The conduits of that influence are your specific strengths, talents, and skills. Remember the strengths, talents, and skills we discussed in the discovery section previously? Well, discovering that value was only the first step.

The next step is to focus on developing those strengths, talents, and skills. This should be the primary focus of your leadership development plan which I refer to as value development. Value development is an intentional focus on your growth through the lens of your strengths, talents, and skills, not a random, aimless approach. Yes, growth will be a byproduct of taking in all the great leadership principles and lessons available to us, but if you want to accelerate your growth and results, focus your leadership development efforts through the lens of value development.

> **Value development is an intentional focus on your growth through the lens of your strengths, talents, and skills, not a random, aimless approach.**

Let's envision this for a second. If you were to refer back to your list of strengths, talents, and skills, selecting two to three overall that you would focus on for the next six to twelve months, what impact would they have on your life? Take five minutes to stop and think about this. By consistently developing those targeted strengths, talents, or skills, how far could your habits develop? Concentrating your efforts in this way will lead to greater returns. When you focus on developing your value, you access deeper levels of your potential. This builds on the clarity you've already established in the discovery chapter.

Here's an example using my own development journey. During my discovery zone, I realized that I was strong in strategy development and good at creating ideas to solve people's problems. In addition, I discovered that I had a talent in creative communication, speaking, and writing, and desired to learn the skill sets of coaching and training. Here's how I focused this value into a value development plan and approach.

My value development plan centered around my strengths, talents, and skills eighty percent of the time, with twenty percent focusing on leadership fundamentals and character development (more universal leadership development). This meant that I spent the majority of my time growing the value I discovered. I took the time to read books on the topics of speaking, coaching, and training. I attended workshops/trainings and found networks with people who had similar strengths, talents, and skills, in addition to anything else that could help me grow.

What you will notice is that the top four currencies in life are at play here: time invested, whether to gain knowledge or join networks of people, and money invested into more resources to help me develop my value. This is the key to developing the value you've discovered. You must guard, measure, and manage your time spent, seek out all the knowledge you can find that will help you grow in the two to three strengths, talents, or skills you've chosen, then, join a network of like-minded people. And always be willing to invest money into your value development.

There you have it, that's really the blueprint for how you can develop your value. Now, assess how you will apply this to your life. I gave you an example from my life as a reference point; however, this won't stick until you begin practicing this in your own. You must consistently assess yourself, focusing on the growth of your strong areas. This development will increase your value contribution which will enlarge your capacity as a leader.

In my personal experience, having a concentrated focus on developing my strengths completely transformed my mentality and approach to leadership development. It accelerated my growth and results. The same will happen for you if you apply this approach to your life. Quit trying to master every leadership principle under the sun. Instead, focus on obtaining every drop of potential hidden within the value of your strengths, talents, and skills.

Let's review the practical steps of how you can accomplish this in your life:

→ First, establish a baseline. What is the current level of each strength, talent, and skill? Go through your list, rating each on a scale of one through ten, indicating where you are in your development journey.
→ Then, for each strength, talent, and skill, write down what you are doing well and where there is room for improvement. (Don't judge yourself; the key is awareness.)
→ Next, pick only two to three areas you will focus on for your improvement or development plan.
→ Determine the habits necessary for improvement or development to occur. What actions should you be doing daily? Remember to focus on process here.

→ Break these habits down into your daily and weekly schedule for the next three to six months. Focusing on only two to three areas makes this doable.

The key is to start small, keeping in mind that value development is a continuous process not a destination (outcome). Over time, you will experience less of those frustrating cycles where you decide to improve or develop an area of your life, only to see your efforts fall off into the same old inconsistency. The morale boost alone from small process-based wins is intoxicating enough to motivate you towards greater outcomes of value development.

The key is to start small, keeping in mind that value development is a continuous process not a destination (outcome).

High-Capacity Leaders Prioritize Their Life.

A professor stood before his philosophy class with some items in front of him. When the class began, wordlessly, he picked up a very large and empty mayonnaise jar and proceeded to fill it with golf balls. He asked the students if the jar was full. They agreed that it was.

The professor then picked up a box of pebbles and poured them into the jar. He shook the jar lightly. The pebbles rolled into the open areas between the golf balls. When he asked the students again if the jar was full, they agreed it was.

The professor next picked up a box of sand and poured it into the jar. Of course, the sand filled up everything else, so He asked once more if the jar was full. The students responded with a unanimous, "Yes."

Finally, the professor produced two glasses of red wine from under the table and poured the entire contents into the jar, effectively filling the empty space between the grains of sand. The students laughed. As the laughter subsided, the professor proceeded to explain to them what I'm going to explain to you.

The jar represents your life. We've all, at some point, felt the pressures of that jar: trying to figure out how to fit it all in, how to meet the demands that every priority brings. Imagine if this professor put the pebbles in first; then the golf balls, which represent larger priorities, would not have fit. A critical step in becoming a high-capacity leader is establishing your priorities, or as my mother might say, get your priorities straight! This ensures that you are clear on what matters most, and intentional in how you distribute your value.

THE IMPORTANCE OF PRIORITIZING

Why is prioritization so important? Research demonstrates the importance of prioritizing our lives. If you're interested in more extensive research regarding this topic, I recommend a simple Google search. For our purposes, though, I want to direct your attention to three major reasons why prioritization is important.

Effectiveness

Prioritizing your life will increase your effectiveness. Let's be honest; there are results you desire in your life. We humans are built with a reward system ingrained within our being. Therefore, we receive a great boost in confidence when we are able to measure the degree to which we are successful at producing a desired result. Prioritizing your life allows you to become more effective.

Limited Distractions

Have you ever felt burned out? Like there are just too many expectations, requests, responsibilities, demands, etc.? Burnout takes place when we are forced into what I call a *reactionary state* versus a *prioritized state*. The reactionary state takes place when the important things and the not so important things are so mixed up that we can't determine which is which. Therefore, we attempt to respond to it all. Prioritizing your life will help you limit the distractions and better determine what to say "no" to! Although this sounds simple, it is a huge milestone. Remember, much of your success will be determined by what you say "no" to versus when you say "yes." Having clearly defined priorities allows you to know which is which.

MIT

This acronym is often used in business. It stands for "most important thing." The final, and greatest importance of prioritizing your life is ensuring the most important things in your life occupy the best of your attention and time. How sad would it be to spend your entire life ineffective at giving your best to the most important priorities because you were distracted? "Keep the main thing the main thing," as they say. Set your priorities; then, the rest just becomes sand. The remainder of this chapter will provide a framework to help you identify the main things and keep the main things at the top of your priority list.

How we organize our priorities will determine what fits.

Let's refer back to our opening story. Just like the jar in this story, how we organize our priorities will determine what fits. If we put the pebbles of our life as the most important thing, then we will limit the capacity for everything else to fit. The same is true when it comes to the distribution of the value you've taken the time to discover and now develop. Value development must be accompanied by life prioritization. Clearly identifying your priorities will grant you more confidence, peace, fulfillment, and clear life vision. This is the second step in becoming a high-capacity leader.

In the previous section we discussed the importance of developing your value. Now, we shift to the next step which is knowing exactly where to focus your value distribution by incorporating a framework I call the *7 Priorities of High-Capacity Leaders*. These are the seven most important priorities in life, and they provide a foundation for effective value distribution. You can see them in the chart below.

7 Priorities of High-Capacity Leaders
1. Personal Devotion
2. Family
3. Community
4. Profession
5. Finance
6. Mental Health
7. Physical Health

These are listed in order of MIT (most important thing), emphasizing God, knowledge, and relationships at the top. You may not agree with the list of priorities I've provided. That is okay; I encourage you to do what you believe is best for your life. The priorities I've listed are rooted in biblical principles, supported by centuries of historical evidence in addition to that found in the scientific study of human behavior. However, as an organizational psychologist who advocates for everyone doing their own research and measurement test, I believe each should test for themselves the effectiveness of their priority list. Now, let's discuss the importance of each priority.

Personal Devotion

Devotion is defined as a love or enthusiasm for a person, activity, or cause. Devotion is the top priority in life. We are all devoted to something or someone. Whatever sits in the first spot will be the main focus of your life. For example, if your physical health were holding down the one spot, then every area of your life would be filtered through that lens. From the moment you woke up, your focus might be how good you look and what you need to put into your body to continue growing and looking this good. The most important thing when it came to your family would be their physical health. Your community would be filled with like-minded people who also have their physical health as the number one priority. Physical health would influence your work days and profession, in addition to where you spend a large amount of your finances. Is any of that bad? Absolutely not! The point here is that whatever you place in the number one spot will influence and set the tone for the rest of your priorities.

The same would be true if finance were in the first spot. From the moment you opened your eyes, finance would be the focus. How and where can I make more money? Your community would be represented by like-minded financially focused people. The primary focus of your profession would be money. Your mental and physical health would suffer when you weren't hitting your financial goals. You wouldn't show up well for your marriage or family when finances weren't going well. I think you get the picture now. The number one spot represents top priority. Whatever sits in this spot is your devotion and will dictate how you prioritize your time, knowledge, network, and money, ultimately determining your mentality and experience in life. Yes, the number one spot is that important!

As I shared previously, faith is the foundation of my life. Therefore, for me, personal devotion is top priority in my life. It's what dictates the tone of my day, how I spend my time, where I gain knowledge and wisdom, how I determine the network and communities to take part in, and more. When this area is out of whack, so follows the other six priorities of my life. Personal devotion is the most important priority because it prioritizes eternal value. This forces me to evaluate my lifestyle from an eternal perspective which guides my values and decisions.

I've tried every other person, place, or thing in that top spot, and NONE have produced a return like prioritizing God first. Some of the greatest leaders of our time have attributed their success to their spiritual life. Personal devotion is the number one priority for a high-capacity leader! Why? Because those who are entrusted with distributing high value across multiple priorities can't endure without the supernatural hand, wisdom, and knowledge of God. Many have tried without God and failed miserably. High-capacity leaders know that their power source is the Lord.

> **I've tried every other person, place, or thing in that top spot, and NONE have produced a return like prioritizing God first.**

You may be wondering, *What is personal devotion, and what does an example of prioritizing God first even look and feel like?* Personal devotion is a designated quiet time that you spend praying, reading God's Word, worshiping, and ultimately reflecting on your relationship with God. Here's an example. A well-executed day for me begins with spending the first of my day (usually thirty to sixty minutes) with God: reading my Bible, taking in the knowledge, wisdom, direction, love, grace, joy, and strength of the gospel. I might meditate in worship, allowing space for the heavy areas of my life and mental health to be lifted and restored or pray, sitting there talking to God, thanking God for everything I can think of being grateful for, sharing my worries, fears, doubts, frustrations, etc. This is the best part of my day and sets the foundation for a tremendous return right at the start of my day.

Do what you believe is best for you; just remember that whatever sits in that first spot will position as the main priority of your life. So, the question is this: what or who currently occupies your number one spot? Really take a moment and think about, based on your actions, what you give your time to first every day. Or pay attention this week, and identify your number one priority, and how it impacts the other areas of your life? The goal here—once again—is awareness, not judgment. Be completely honest with what you uncover. What influence does your number one priority have on the rest of your priorities and overall life? Is it a positive impact? Articulate your results whether it be through conversation, your journal, or speaking out loud to yourself if you are serious about measuring your top priority.

Family

High-capacity leaders make family their second greatest priority. In my best Vin Diesel voice I say to you, "What's real is family!" (I bet you didn't think you would get a *Fast and Furious* reference while reading this book.) In all seriousness, though, family is second because it's truly what's real. It's where we should give and receive the second greatest amount of value in our life. That value is in the form of unconditional love. Family is where we can be vulnerable, broken, silly, unprofessional, crazy, highly challenged and most importantly, real.

If you want proof of the power and benefits of family, look no further than the fact that this entire thing we call the human race began with one family. Even if you don't believe that, one thing you can't deny is that at the root of any group we consider family you will find an abundance of love. Family teaches us how to give and receive the greatest gift—unconditional love. This type of love is special because it's not limited by our human defects. In other words, when it comes to family, our flaws don't limit their love (or at least they shouldn't). Prioritizing family increases the value and distribution of love in your life. The desire to be loved is something we are all born with; family should contribute to satisfying this need.

Both personal devotion and family are eternally valuable. Each priority involves giving and receiving value that extends beyond our time on this earth; that's the beauty of eternal value. Think about this. As a high-capacity leader in your family, the unconditional love and leadership you provide can extend for generations. Your son, grandson, great-grandson, etc., will carry a piece of your legacy. High-capacity leaders pass down large pieces of legacy.

How are you currently adding and receiving value in your family? This is something to constantly monitor and consider. The goal is not perfection. There will be moments where you slip off track and family takes a back seat; however, these priorities are meant to serve as a true north when the alignment of your life is off. For those of you who don't have any blood ties or maybe there's conflict within your actual family, don't worry. This applies to whoever you've entrusted with the functions and privilege of being considered your family.

Community

We are better together than we are alone. We were not created to live in isolation. You were specifically designed to desire, flourish, advance, develop, and prosper from having a relationship with others. I assure you that you are the best version of yourself when you prioritize experiencing all of life's highs and lows with others. We all need community. I'll say that again for greater emphasis, we all need community!

Think about the worldwide phenomenon of social media. Why do you think such a simple concept of giving people access to meet other people at a rapid rate has grown into a multibillion dollar industry? It's because we crave community. Like adding more logs of wood to a fire, so is the impact of adding community to your life. Your passion, vibrance, and sense of life will brighten like an open flame when you prioritize community. I want to be very clear, though. I am referring to healthy communities. Not all communities are healthy. A large number of people does not equal a large amount of value. And, I would like to point out that community and network are one and the same. Therefore, consider the following list as a continuation of the list provided in the network section. If you're curious what makes a healthy community, consider these elements:

→ Support.

High-capacity leaders give and receive encouragement and support from their community. Imagine being surrounded by people who are all at different stages of life yet committed to helping, encouraging, serving, and supporting one another. Doesn't this sound like an ideal environment? This is what happens in a healthy community. People seek to support and encourage one another, carry each other's burdens, and leverage their life experience to help those who are going through situations they've already overcome. It's truly a cycle of service. High-capacity leaders not only contribute to this type element of community but they build supportive and encouraging communities.

→ Fun.

If you were to count the moments where you have the highest number of laughs and fun, community should be near or at the top of that list! A healthy community is anything but boring or stressful. You should enjoy time spent with your community. Whether you're eating, meeting, or worshiping together, fun should be present! High-capacity leaders know how to join in and/or start the fun because they understand that this is a vital piece of community.

→ Ministry.

Matthew 18:20 tells us that God is present when we gather in community to minister to each other. Think about that for a second. This fact alone tells us how valuable even

God considers it. The fact that God would want to join in speaks of its importance. Ministry may seem like a heavy religious term, but I'd like to challenge you to think of it this way. Ministering to others has a tremendous impact on faith, whether that's faith in yourself, faith in others, or faith in God. That's powerful! Faith translates into hope, which impacts our outlook on the future, resulting in a more fulfilling life! That's the power of a strong community ministry. High-capacity leaders prioritize community because, there, they experience ministry.

→ Love.

There's nothing like experiencing an entire community of love. I could write a million words about this point, yet none of it would compare to experiencing it for yourself. Let's face it; for all of us, there are times where we experience low days, down moments, moments we may not want to even share with our family. This is where being a part of a loving community becomes invaluable. You can't weather the storms of life alone; you need the love that generates within a strong, healthy community. High-capacity leaders understand this and look to spread love as well as receive love. It's a beautiful thing!

→ Growth.

Iron sharpens iron is a well-known proverb that couldn't be more true when we think about the benefits and importance of community. I covered this a bit in the currency section regarding networks, so I won't elaborate extensively here. What I will reemphasize, though, is if you're looking to accelerate your growth in any of the other six priorities, nothing advances growth quicker than community. It's the secret weapon of a high-capacity leader.

Profession

Our profession represents how we add value in the marketplace. This is the priority that many are most familiar with. For a high-capacity leader, profession is more of a playground than an obligation forced upon us in order to provide for self and others. High-capacity leaders understand that the goal of this priority is to earn capital through serving, with the ultimate purpose of buying back as much time, knowledge, and network as possible. Remember that those are the top three currencies in life. We work to own our time, gain more knowledge, and to increase our service while building and contributing to other high value networks.

High-capacity leaders thrive in the marketplace. Why? Because they've made it through the discovery zone and constantly focus on developing the value they've discovered. This leads to successfully accomplishing a clear understanding of how they best serve, establishing themselves as highly respected experts in their fields. This achievement transforms their experience while serving in the marketplace. As Rick Warren says, "Nothing becomes dynamic, until it becomes clear."[4] Our professional life gains a massive amount of clarity when we understand who we are and how we best serve with the value we've been given. How are you serving in the marketplace? High-capacity leaders give and receive value in the marketplace.

---

4 Rick, Warren, "How to Move from Managing to Leading Your Church," *Married People For Churches*, 6 Dec. 2018, https://marriedpeoplechurches.org/author/rick-warren/.

> **High-capacity leaders thrive in the marketplace because they've made it through the discovery zone and constantly focus on developing the value they've discovered.**

Finance

This is one of my favorite priorities. Why? Because once you have the other four priorities aligned, money becomes attracted to you. That's right; high-capacity leaders know how to leverage their value in the marketplace. This ensures that all their needs and the majority of their wants are taken care of. That describes a blessed life! Raise your hand if you would like to experience a blessed life.

Unfortunately, the data reveals that most Americans aren't enjoying a blessed financial life due to the lack of prioritizing financial literacy. Check out some of these American financial literacy statistics:

- → The average score on the US national financial literacy test hovers around 68 percent.
- → Money management is among the most requested classes by high schoolers in the US.
- → Most Americans give wrong answers to investing, setting personal financial goal, and credit-building questions.
- → A lack of financial knowledge can lead to fewer employment opportunities.
- → Nearly one-fifth of US teens haven't learned fundamental financial skills.

→ College education doesn't guarantee a better financial future.
→ Only twelve percent of millennials have asked for professional help with personal finances.

High-capacity leaders understand the importance of financial literacy; therefore, they focus on adding to their financial knowledge (there's that second greatest currency again) and managing their finances. This gives them the opportunity to lead with capital (small or large).

Mental Health

Our mental space is the hub, the central headquarters of our being. High-capacity leaders prioritize their mental health. They understand that this helps to overcome the three seeds of limitation we spoke about earlier (fear, doubt, and inaction). Prioritizing our mental health guards our life against the many lies attacking our heart, which is the seat of our emotions, self-worth, and trust.

As I write this, the topic of mental health has become a common discussion. Experts and society at large have realized how important it should be and the silent impact it has had on many men and women, struggling to balance all of the responsibilities of life. One best practice high-capacity leaders exercise in order to add, receive, and manage the value of their mental health is something I like to call *gateway guarding*. The gateways I am referring to are the five portals to our mind: environment, eyes, ears, expression, and experience. Guarding these gateways helps to keep a healthy mental space. Below, I've highlighted two of these portals and why it's important that we consciously maintain our guard.

→ Eyes

The lamp of the body is the eye. If your eye is good, your whole body will be full of light. But if your eye is bad, your whole body will be full of darkness (Matthew 6:22). Our eyes provide a portal to our mind. High-capacity leaders guard this portal, understanding that what we set our eyes on has a tremendous impact on our mental health.

I remember firsthand the impact of this portal during 2020 when there was a tremendous amount of unrest socially, due to the racial tension cutting through our nation. The images of young men and women who look like me sharing their unfortunate experiences, some sharing similar experiences to my own life, left a mark on me. I began to notice the impact these images had on me mentally. I felt heavy and angry, among many other emotions, and all this affected my productivity and focus. Eventually, I had to turn it off and concentrate my attention on more effective energy.

It's important to note here that I'm not advocating burying one's head in the sand in an effort to guard your eyes and maintain a healthy mental space. What you should take from this is the importance of balance, translating what you see quickly into productive actions and healthy outlets.

Have you ever turned on the TV and watched something that moved you emotionally? Whether that moment was positive or negative isn't the point. I want to draw your attention to the impact an electronic box of sounds and images can have on your life. Whether you're watching the news (good luck with that), internet, entertainment, social media, or any other visual stimuli, it's important that high-capacity leaders are mindful of the effect this portal has on mental health. They add, receive, and manage the value that flows through this portal in order to maintain a healthy mental space.

→ Expression

This word can represent the production of something. Every day we have mental expressions produced by our internal and external voice. What we say to ourselves and even to others can have a tremendous impact on the life cycle of our mental health. The dialogue we allow internally or externally has the power of life and death. Although this statement may sound a bit extreme, many scientific studies have proven this statement to be true.

One particular experiment that comes to mind was an experiment conducted by IKEA demonstrating how negativity can stop growth. The team at IKEA filmed the effect of negative words—compared to compliments—on a plant. Here's an excerpt from the study:

IKEA asked students at GEMS Wellington Academy in Dubai to record a load of insults and compliments. It then took two plants and gave them both the exact same conditions in terms of the amount of sunlight and water, but they altered what the plants "listened" to. The "bullied" plant was played recordings of negative, hurtful comments, such as, "You're not even green," and "You look rotten." The other plant listened to recordings of positive comments like, "Seeing you blossom makes me happy." They played the comments on a loop for a period of thirty days. The plant receiving positive messages remained healthy; however, the one which was played all the negative comments simply wilted and became discolored. Some people have said this is a similar effect to that which impacts victims of bullying. And we couldn't think of a better way to educate people.[5]

IKEA isn't the first to test out this hypothesis. The point here is high-capacity leaders guard the portal of their internal and external expressions. Making sure that their internal and external dialogue are life-giving not negative, hurtful, or self-limiting. The other two portals focus on what we listen to in addition to our surroundings. As you can imagine, these portals have just as much an impact and are the reason why mental health must be a priority.

Physical Health

We've only been given one body, so it's important that we take care of it. Now, I would be the first to say that if I didn't have a wife who prioritizes my seeing a doctor from time to time (every five years), I would probably never see the doctor. I know many of you reading this are just like me, and that's not good. In fact, a Cleveland Clinic study found that we men will do almost anything to avoid going to the doctor. Here are some of the statistics:[6]

→ For 1,174 US males eighteen years or older, Cleveland Clinic found that 72 percent of men would rather do household chores, like cleaning the bathroom or mowing the lawn, than go to the doctor.
→ 20 percent of men admit they have not been completely honest with their doctor before.

---

5 Jessica, Jones, "Ikea Asks People to Bully This Plant for 30 Days to See What Happens, and Results Are Eye-opening," *Bored Panda*, 13 Jan. 2019, https://www.boredpanda.com/ikea-experiment-bully-a-plant-jessica-ones/?utm_source=google&utm_medium=organic&utm_campaign=organic.

6 Tracy Wheeler, "Cleveland Clinic Survey: Men Will Do Almost Anything to Avoid Going to the Doctor," *Cleveland Clinic Newsroom*, 5 Sept. 2019, https://newsroom.clevelandclinic.org/2019/09/04/cleveland-clinic-survey-men-will-do-almost-anything-to-avoid-going-to-the-doctor/.

- → 36 percent didn't want to hear that they needed to change their diet/lifestyle.
- → 37 percent they knew something was wrong but weren't ready to face the diagnosis and/or would rather not know if they had any health issues.
- → 41 percent were told as children that men don't complain about health issues.
- → 82 percent of men try to stay healthy to live longer for friends and family who rely on them, yet only 50 percent engage in preventative care.

Prioritizing one's health is very important. As a high-capacity leader, I'd like to challenge us all to prioritize our health. I'm talking specifically to the men on this one. The ladies tend to do a better job; let's learn from them.

As you probably noticed, the priorities we just reviewed, all revolve around adding, receiving, or managing value across the most important areas in life. For some, you may find yourself demonstrating all three (adding, receiving, and managing). For others, you may only operate in one of the three. The importance is to be aware of how you're adding value, constantly measuring effectiveness, future goals, and present habits. This is how you create a development plan for your life.

Here's an example. Say you put together a plan for the next two months across all priorities. First, determine whether your main focus will be on adding, receiving, managing value, or all the above. Early on, only select one of the three as you build your plan. This value-centered focus will have a tremendous impact on your development and life overall.

In the exercise below, I've provided an example of what a sixty-day development plan would entail.

7 Priorities of High-Capacity Leaders	Value (added or received)	Goal	Habit (Process)	Results: First 30 days
1) Personal Devotion	Receive: Spend time with God daily	30 minutes per day first thing in the morning	Must wake up 40 minutes earlier than usual	Stronger focus, increased hope, clarity of future, increased confidence
2) Family	Add: Dedicate quality time to wife and son	Saturday morning trip to downtown Sanford with the family. Dance in the kitchen with son after dinner	Lock in a calendar date with wife invited. Turn on "out of office" at 4 pm	Stronger marriage, special memories, great example for son of work/life balance
3) Community	Manage: Connect with close friends (been awhile). Add: Serve friends	Book a date to visit the driving range with friends next Thursday. Find out where I can add value to their lives	Reach out on Monday morning. Ask during driving range visit how I can serve/help friends	Build stronger relationships and trust with people I value
4) Profession				
5) Finance				
6) Mental Health				
7) Physical Health				

Now that you've had the opportunity to analyze the previous example, it's your turn. Complete the next chart, and create an example of what a development plan could look like for your life.

If you find it challenging to complete an example of your own plan, don't worry. Getting this perfect the first time is not the goal. The cool thing about this plan is that it grows with you. Therefore, there's no pressure on getting this right in the beginning. Now for some less encouraging truth. Your plan will have moments of failure! You will get all excited about waking up earlier, changing habits, gaining more activity, and then BAM! One day failure will smack you right between the eyes.

> **Your plan will have moments of failure! You will get all excited about waking up earlier, changing habits, gaining more activity, and then BAM! One day failure will smack you right between the eyes.**

I'm being overly dramatic here, but you get my point. I need to emphasize something here. As unpleasant as those moments of failure sound, know that it is perfectly normal. It's a regular element of the growth process; therefore, don't become discouraged when those inevitable challenges arise. Remember process over outcomes. The key with your development plan is to lock onto the process. Maybe you don't go big with every priority; maybe only focus on major change in two to three priorities and add incremental habit shifts in the other three to four. Look back at the example, and notice that I only focus major goals around personal devotion, family, and profession. Because three of the remaining four areas already have a healthy projection, my attention there will be smaller.

7 Priorities Of High-Capacity Leaders	Value (added or received)	Goal	Habit	Results
1) Personal Devotion				
2) Family				
3) Community				
4) Profession				
5) Finance				
6) Mental Health				
7) Physical Health				

I believe we are all called to become high-capacity leaders. While we may not all lead in the same capacity, the development zone requires that we all take the same approach to determining how we develop our value and prioritize our lives. Remember: process is key in this zone as development is an ongoing process.

With that being said, I still strongly encourage you to capture the milestones of your development. This is critically important to your morale as a leader. Gaining a return on your value and prioritizing value distribution in your life is not an easy task. While the points in this chapter seem simple, I am not naive to the difficulty of execution in this zone. This zone took me years to figure out; therefore, don't be discouraged if it seems a bit overwhelming in one sitting. Start where you are, and maintain a long-term view. What's that starting point for you? You may spend this entire year simply working on the alignment of your personal devotion or professional skills you'd like to gain proficiency and expertise in.

I use a year as an example; however, this could be several years. Again, this is why *a process-centered focus is so important*. Becoming a high-capacity leader is just that, becoming. It means that this is who you are—not something you accomplish. Becoming speaks to the process of growth; therefore, give yourself grace as you navigate the exercises in this chapter.

Think of this work as the beginnings of establishing your legacy. Stop here, and focus on putting in the work. In the next chapter, we will expand on the impact that developing your value and priorities has on your decisions.

REFLECTION

1) What is your greatest takeaway from this chapter?

2) Which points should you go back and review?

3) What were the most challenging points in this chapter? Why?

4) How will this chapter impact your life moving forward?

5) Find someone to share your new development plan with. Who will this person be, and when will you be sharing with them?

CHAPTER 4

DECISIONS: THE LAND OF CLARITY

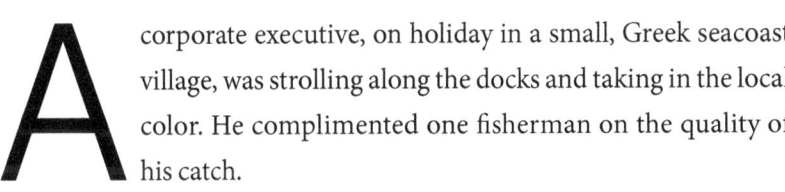

A corporate executive, on holiday in a small, Greek seacoast village, was strolling along the docks and taking in the local color. He complimented one fisherman on the quality of his catch.

"How long did it take you to get all those fish?" he asked.

"Not very long," answered the Greek. "An hour or two."

"Then why didn't you stay out longer to catch more?"

Shrugging, the Greek explained that his catch was sufficient to meet his needs and those of his family.

The executive asked, "But what do you do with the rest of your time?"

The fisherman answered, "I sleep late, fish a little, play with my children, and take a nap with my wife. In the evening, I go to the village to see my friends, dance a little, play the bouzouki, and sing songs. I have a full life."

The executive said, "Well I have an MBA from Harvard, and I'm sure I can help you. You should start by fishing longer every day. You'll catch extra fish that you can sell. With the revenue, you can buy a bigger boat. With the extra money the larger boat will bring you, you can buy a second boat and a third one, and so on, until you have an entire fleet of trawlers. Instead of selling your fish to a middle man, you can then negotiate directly with the processing plants and maybe even open your own plant. You can ship fish to markets all around the world. In time, you can then move to New York City to direct your huge enterprise."

"How long would that take?" asked the Greek.

"Twenty, perhaps twenty-five years," replied the executive.

"And after that?"

"When your business gets really big, you can sell stock and make millions!" exclaimed the executive with zeal.

"Millions? Really? And after that?"

"After that you'll be able to retire, live in a small village near the coast, sleep late, play with your grandchildren, catch a few fish, take a nap with your wife, and spend your evenings singing, dancing, and playing the bouzouki with your friends."

DECISION-MAKING IS A CRITICAL SKILL.

This story paints the perfect depiction of why decision-making is a critical skill. The fisherman's life represents a life searched, demonstrating the peace and fulfillment that accompanies completing the journey from dreams, to discovery, then development, before finally arriving at the zone of decisions. On the other hand, some might paint a negative outlook of the executive. I don't think that's necessary.

> **The executive's only mistake in this story was assuming that his definition of success was the same as the fisherman's.**

The executive's only mistake in this story was assuming that his definition of success was the same as the fisherman's. A fulfilled life for the fisherman involved sleeping late, fishing a little, playing with his children, and taking a nap with his wife. Then, in the evenings, going to the village to see friends, dancing a little, playing the bouzouki, and singing songs. This did not represent fulfillment for the executive, and that's okay.

In the discovery section, I had you answer questions regarding your values, identifying what's important to you. This is critical because, with every decision, there comes a sacrifice. By choosing one thing, you inevitably give up another. While the executive was right—the fisherman could've made a ton of money by advancing his fishing business—the fisherman already possessed a firm grasp of his values, skills, strengths, talents, and priorities. He knew that if he chose the life the executive described, he would miss out on the things that mattered the most to him. The ability to make great decisions not only equips us to take advantage of life-changing opportunities, it also saves us from sacrificing what matters most. As Cal Newport says: "Clarity of what matters, also provides clarity of what doesn't."[7]

THE POWER OF CLARITY

Decisions are the exam of life. Each day, you are faced with a multitude of choices that either feed the greatness within you or pull you farther away from your destiny! Welcome to the management portion of life. From this point forward, the goal is to simplify important decisions. The most exciting thing about the zone of decisions, is that in this zone you finally begin to experience fulfillment. This is often because you now know what areas lead to a life filled with purpose, like the fisherman in the opening story.

Hopefully by now you have become keenly aware of the systems that will be required to maintain and manage a fulfilling life. Decision-making is easy once you know which dreams to pursue and when, have discovered what your strengths, skills, and talents are, and have a clear understanding of your priorities, along with a plan for continuous growth. The decision zone is the land of clarity because clarity of vision derives from greater heights in understanding who you are, what you're made of, and how you best serve. This increased sense of direction will have a tremendous impact on your overall sense of purpose. It will also make you more resilient, increasing your ability to bounce back from setbacks,

---

[7] Cal Newport, "Quote by Cal Newport," *Deepstash*, https://deepstash.com/idea/11620/clarity-about-what-matters-provides-clarity-about-what-does-not.

disappointments, failures, and delayed gratification! Let's explore this zone a bit further.

The word "decide" comes from the Latin word *cis*, which means "to cut off or kill." Translated into our lives, this could be represented as knowing the right door to enter or the right door to close—decisions concerning friendships, entertainment, education, thoughts, actions, values, etc.! Have you ever wavered in your commitments either to yourself or others? When faced with large decisions, are you able to decisively choose what to do, and then do it, or do you often get stuck wrestling with uncertainty? If you wrestle, for the remainder of this chapter, I would like to equip you with a few tools that will help you further solidify your decision-making abilities.

The major decisions in your life will fall into one of three categories: performance-based decisions, priority-based decisions, and principle-based decisions. As you read through the details of each decision category, I encourage you to use all three categories as criteria when needing to break down important decisions in your life.

PERFORMANCE-BASED DECISIONS

Performance-based decisions involve making decisions based on your skills, strengths, talents, habits, process, or development plan. Therefore, when you're making a decision that involves any of these elements, it is important to analyze how each element will impact the results of your decision. This may seem like quite a bit, so let's break this down. Here's an example of what performance-based decision-making looks like.

Before my transition out of the corporate space into owning my own business, I had to assess this decision using performance-based decision criteria. In the months leading up to this change, I asked myself this question, *If I'm going to build a successful business, what skills strengths, talents, habits, processes, and development plan will I need to achieve this goal?* I assessed each one of these areas taking note of my strong areas, as well as the challenge areas presenting an opportunity for growth.

> **If I'm going to build a successful business, what skills strengths, talents, habits, processes, and development plan will I need to achieve this goal?**

Applying this performance-based decision criteria helped me realize before becoming a business owner that I would need to acquire and/or adopt new skills, habits, processes and development plans. For instance, prior to becoming a business owner I never had to sell anything. The focus requirement in corporate business was different than the focus required as a sole business owner. Because of this awareness, I made the wise decision of paying for sales training, ordering top sales books, increasing my knowledge around how to acquire elite level focus in my daily work, resulting in elite level production in my business.

What if I had never considered these things? What if I had never applied the performance-based decision criteria? The truth is I may have still transitioned successfully; however, a scarier truth is that I may have underestimated this transition which would have led to a series of terrible decisions and experience.

Think about this in your own life. How often do we just jump into things because they're exciting, because they're new, or because they give us a greater sense of hope? There's nothing wrong with being excited about an upcoming transition or season in your life. I would caution you, though, to filter important decisions through the performance-based decision criteria. Before you make the decision, consider: *Does this align with my skills, strengths, or talents? Does my life currently possess the habitual infrastructure it would take to be successful after making this decision? Have I invested at all into planning this, so that I am set up to excel?*

These are just some of the prompts to consider when working through a major decision. What you will notice is that you won't be able to answer these questions without doing the work required in the discovery zone. Do you see how these zones build on each other? Unpacking your skills, talents, and strengths provides a benchmark for measuring growth and performance.

PRIORITY-BASED DECISIONS

The priorities I am referencing here are the 7 Priorities of a High-Capacity Leader. One of the major benefits of adopting the seven priorities is that they provide a simplified reference point when faced with a big decision that challenges your priorities. A great example would be the one we've already covered in the opening story. The fisherman clearly had his priorities in order long before that executive showed up on the dock. The fisherman had already decided before this interaction that the highest priorities in his life were his family, friends, and naps.

Learn from the fisherman's example, and be sure to solidify your priority list. That way, when an unexpected opportunity approaches the dock of your life, you are prepared to resist the temptation of giving in to any distractions that don't align with your priorities. Remember, much of your success will be determined by what you say "no" to versus what you say "yes" to. I emphasize this point because it is not easy to say "no" to things that seem like a great opportunity.

For those of you reading this who are very talented and capable of doing a wide variety of good things, this temptation will be the greatest for you. I know because I am just like you. However, my life and production went to the next level when a coach of mine sat me down and shared this truth with me. Much like the fisherman, the decisions I was considering were not bad decisions. In fact, they were good opportunities to advance my career. I was faced with the option of starting my own business or pursuing a higher-paying job with a lot of exposure, doing what I do best as a professional. Not a bad choice at all right?

Some may wonder why I didn't pursue that job. After all, owning a business can leave you in a tight spot financially and overworked professionally. The reason why I decided to focus on writing this book and launching my organizational psychology firm (among other endeavors) was a direct result of working through the dreams, discover, and development zone. My dream before entering the corporate world was to run my own business one day. In order to activate that dream, though, I first had to discover the skills, strengths, and talents that would be serviceable in the marketplace, then develop that value while establishing a strong sense of my priorities as I grew.

All this made my decision-making process easier when I was faced with doing the scary thing. (Believe me, passing up a good job is always a bit scary!) Although it was the harder route, I knew, based on the work done in the previous three zones, that it was the right decision. I pay it forward by sharing this with you now. Don't be afraid to say "no" to things even when they seem like good opportunities. If it doesn't align with your priorities or distracts away from the most important things in your life, then there's a really good chance it is not for you.

Furthermore, doing the scary thing can be nerve-racking—especially those moments when people around you aren't aware of your priorities and encourage you to make a decision based on their priorities, just like the executive leader in the opening story. When these pressure situations arise, as they often do, you will have your priorities aligned, ensuring that you make the right decision.

PRINCIPLE-BASED DECISIONS

Principle-based decisions are rooted in a fundamental truth, proposition, or value that serves as a foundation for a system of beliefs, behavior, or chain of events. When you compromise your principles, you jeopardize your ability to make effective decisions. All of the decision-making criteria are important; however, out of the three, this particular criterion is the one that stands out to me the most. Every poor decision I've ever made in my life, when I look back and review the process, has had one thing in common. Each decision involved me compromising my principles.

Any value that can't stand the test of tough or major decisions, isn't a value at all; it's just a nice thought.

Any value that can't stand the test of tough or major decisions, isn't a value at all; it's just a nice thought. If you and I are going to increase our decision-making ability, we have to commit to rejecting the opportunity to compromise the fundamental values in our life. What we value and believe will have the greatest impact on our behavior and results. Being dishonest out of fear of consequence or lowering your standards of integrity when no one is looking can have a detrimental impact on your decision-making ability. Remember, our values shape the decisions we make, and the decisions we make shape the world we live in.

Principle-based decisions have a lasting impact on our lives for better or worse. One memory that comes to mind took place when I was a child. I was just getting into sports and was allowed to play Mighty Mite football. I didn't have much experience, so stepping out on the field was very scary for me. I remember taking a helmet to the knee during a collision and how painful that moment was. This affirmed the fear I was already battling of playing the sport. Therefore, when the pain subsided and my mother asked me how my knee felt, I lied. I told her it was still in pain when it wasn't. I pretended like that temporary injury had a lasting impact.

Because of this lie, I was able to avoid playing the remainder of that season, sidestepping the real issue, which was fear. That wasn't all, though, because of this lie, my mother made the decision to never let me play football again until I was a junior in high school. The point I don't want you to miss here is that my decision to lie violated a principle that cost me years of consequence. Even once I overcame the fear and wanted to get back out there on the field, I couldn't. All because I wasn't honest.

Now, you may be thinking this is a bit over dramatic, and on one hand, yes, my life didn't suffer from not being able to play. However, I want you to translate this story into your own life. What if I had simply made a principle-based decision and shared with my mother that I was really more afraid than hurt? What if the next time you are tempted to forgo your integrity, bypass your values, or give in to compromise, you instead commit to making a principle-based decision? How much more effective would your decisions be; what kind of results would you experience compared to past decisions?

What we value and believe has the greatest impact on our behavior, decisions, and results. I think about this often when a decision of mine doesn't align with the principles, values, and beliefs I claim. I hope that by reading this you will assess the alignment in your life. If you find that your alignment is off, good news, you still have time to make the correction. It is never too late to improve your decision-making ability.

Hopefully the three decision-making categories will serve as an aide when you are faced with a tough or major decision. Use them when you need to break down your choices. If a decision doesn't check two out of three from the categories explained, then think twice before moving forward on that decision.

The following are additional guidelines for effective decision-making:

Your decisions should be based on truth.
With there being so many different varieties and versions of truth in today's world, I thought it might be best to provide a bit of wisdom on the importance of making sure your decisions are rooted in what you consider to be truth. In order to determine what truth is to you, you have to assess your source of truth. Truth is absolute.

If I were to climb up on the top of a building and proceed to jump off, unless I possess a mechanism to help me fly or float or God's hand divinely intervenes, I am going to hit the ground with a hard thud. Why? Because the truth that governs our earth, known as gravity, is absolute. This idea our society has adopted that everyone can have their own truth is extremely dangerous. Just because we believe something to be true, does not mean it is—in fact—truth. Be careful of the truths you adopt, for from this source, you will make decisions that have a chain reaction on your life and the lives of those around you.

Your decisions should lead you to seek out wise counsel.
Wise counsel is a saving grace I encourage you to cherish. As I look back on my life, where I come from, and how I've gotten to the place I am, it's all highly attributed to all the great wisdom in my circle of friends, mentors, leaders, and coaches. I owe them a tremendous amount of gratitude for helping me identify purpose and define success in my life. It is because of them that *The Mentality of Success* was created.

Don't overlook this; take inventory of the wisdom around you and commit to seeking wise counsel when faced with a tough decision. Know that you may not always agree with it, but do yourself a favor and don't forsake the wisdom in your circle. Good counsel has the ability to protect us from major mistakes, granting us experience beyond our current level of knowledge. Wisdom is as good—if not better—than gold!

Know that you may not always agree with wise counsel, but do yourself a favor and don't forsake the wisdom in your circle.

Your decisions should be made with legacy in mind.
I will expand on the topic of legacy in the upcoming section. For now, I bring up the point of legacy simply to remind you that every decision you make impacts your future and the future of all those who follow you. This is an incredible responsibility. In the previous chapters, I told you that there are people who need the value within you. When it comes to your decisions and the legacy you leave, know that people are counting on your decisions. People's lives will directly be impacted by your decisions. I don't share this with you to add pressure; instead, I share it to increase your awareness and inspire you to think ahead.

LEGACY

If you do these things, you will leave a legacy beyond what you could ever have imagined. Everything we've covered in this book thus far has led to this. Legacy. Truth is, I didn't think much about legacy before my son Nehemiah was born. *The Mentality of Success* was an active thought and practice in my life before my son was born; however, I had not yet made it to the zone of decisions before becoming a father. Up until that point, I was intensely focused on the development zone. That all shifted after my son was born. Something changed in my mentality; my futuristic mind began to focus even more on the future. More importantly, I began to recognize how my current decisions would impact my son's life.

According to *Psychology Today*, it is estimated that adults make approximately thirty-five thousand decisions per day.[8] That's about two thousand decisions per hour. This may sound absurd until you consider all the different types of decisions we have at our disposal: judgments, responses, verbal and non-verbal decisions, comfort, spur-of-the-moment, and many more. Added to that is the fact that just about every decision we make has a cause and effect. These minor decisions may not mean a whole lot within the grand scheme; however, it should encourage all of us to ponder how the critical decisions we make today impact the legacy we create for the future.

One of my favorite demonstrations of this is a theory known as the "Butterfly Effect." Meteorologist Edward Lorenz was popularly known as the person who coined this term. The Butterfly Effect states that something as small as the single flap of a butterfly's wings can cause a big change in the weather pattern of a place somewhere far away. For context, the span of an average butterfly's wings is approximately 30 mm. That's a little over an inch. I don't know about you, but that blows my mind. Something so small—by just the flap of its wings—can create a chain reaction in an entirely different location.

---

[8] Eva M. Krockow, *How Many Decisions Do We Make Each Day? Psychology Today*, 27 Sept. 2018, https://www.psychologytoday.com/us/blog/stretching-theory/201809/how-many-decisions-do-we-make-each-day.

I'm here to tell you that your decisions have an even greater impact. Your decisions affect not only today but also the years ahead. Let's be honest, I'm not telling you anything your mom hasn't lectured you about before; however, I challenge you to absorb what I'm saying from a different, more positive perspective. Become aware of the amazing opportunity you have in front of you. Like me, you may have never thought about your legacy up until this point, but I assure you it's never too early to consider the effect you want to leave on this world.

I shared this because as you work through all four zones, there will come a time when the shift in your mentality will take place the same way mine did. This shift could very well happen for you while single, while in college, or while in high school. The focus on legacy takes place when we become aware of the opportunity we have before us to leave a lasting legacy. If you've never considered it before, take a moment to answer the following question:

What do you want your overall legacy to be?

I once read a book that asked me to write my own eulogy (what I want my friends and family to say once I'm gone). I found this to be extremely weird at first. I nearly skipped over this exercise. Thankfully, I decided to give it a shot. To my surprise, this level of reflection forced me to consider my legacy for the first time, having a profound impact on my life. What impacted me the most was realizing that many of the things I wanted my family, friends, and coworkers to say didn't connect to the daily mark I was living. I had allowed myself to get caught up in the tunnel vision of day-to-day challenges, complacency, and frustration.

So, I invite you to conduct this same exercise as we close this chapter and book. What do you want the people you love to say about you when you're gone? To get the greatest results, write this down somewhere. Keep it and review it every now and then throughout the months and years. Assess whether your life continues to consistently align with the mark you wish to leave.

Now think about your legacy in the following areas.
Personal Devotion

What will your loved ones remember you being devoted to? What will it be? Will it be your job, friends, family, self? What do you want people to remember when it comes to your personal devotion?

Family

What will your legacy be within your family? Whether you're married or single, you equally have the opportunity to leave a family legacy. Think about what you want that to be. For someone single, you may want your parents to remember you as a loving, honorable son. What are you doing today in order to build that legacy?

Community

What impact do you hope to have on your community? This doesn't have to be a large group of people. This could be a small group of friends. The most important thing is determining what mark you want to leave on their lives and building towards it. For me, I've been challenged with this thought as I assess the small amount of time I get to spend with my friends lately. As I write this, we are transitioning out of a worldwide pandemic that has greatly impacted the frequency with which I see my friends. I share this to remind you of the importance of taking advantage of the time given with friends.

Profession

What mark do you wish to leave on the marketplace? How are you building towards this result every day? Think about the people at your place of work or those who conduct business with you. What mark do you wish to leave on these people?

Finance

How will you leave a financial legacy? Many think about this point, yet few take the necessary steps to build one. While this point is often thought about with children in mind, maybe you don't have or want any children. In your case, is there a cause that matters to you and would benefit from your future generosity?

By simply asking these questions, the odds of your leaving a greater legacy increase tremendously. Many of us don't think about them until life has caught up with us, and we are faced with our own mortality. Don't wait until that point before considering the mark all the great value within you can leave. Leaving your mark will be a daily pursuit. You won't always hit the target, so don't fret when that happens. Developing a mentality that consistently considers the mark you make on the world will elevate your decisions, your focus, and your life experience.

Developing a mentality that consistently considers the mark you make on the world will elevate your decisions, your focus, and your life experience.

CONCLUSION

That's it; that's the framework. You are now equipped and ready to define the success your life was created to experience. As we come to a close, I want you to know something. There is no one like you; you are unique in the sense that there has never been a you. This book is so important because your success is vital to this world. My hope is that you now understand that success is a mentality. Much more than what you do or achieve, success is who you are! It's the reason you are here! You were created to succeed.

As you've worked your way through *The Mentality of Success* framework, you should possess a deeper understanding of your value, transforming your outlook on your life and success. You have a roadmap that will help you access the deepest levels of your purpose and potential. With that being said, I leave you with a few final thoughts.

Purpose is a maturation process.
Discovering your purpose can be tough and at times, a frustrating experience. *I thought I wanted this, but now I'm not so sure. I thought I would excel at this, but all I experience is failure.* These are some of the ebbs and

flows that can discourage us from believing that we were created with purpose. From this day forward, shift your mentality, the way you think about your life purpose. Begin to see your purpose as a maturation process, a series of valuable moments, rather than this endless search for a singular peak moment.

> **Begin to see your purpose as a maturation process, a series of valuable moments, rather than this endless search for a singular peak moment.**

Your purpose extends beyond any particular career, status, accomplishment, or feeling. Your purpose is tied to your Creator, family, community, skills, strengths, talents, and so much more! Don't underestimate yourself! You are a complex being and for good reason. You were intricately designed; therefore, managing yourself can feel like a challenging task at times. Be careful not to mistake growth for failure. Fall in love with your maturation process, knowing that purpose equals intent, and your life was definitely intended for success! Take the good with the bad, along with the uncertainty that rivals the fulfilling moments in your life. Why? Because it all counts, and just like you, it all matters.

Dare to live out your dreams.
I know we covered this topic extensively; however, I wanted to give it one final push. Dare to live out your dreams! Be strong and courageous,

knowing that your God-given dreams carry the salt that this world needs. Therefore, activate those dreams by taking hold of the authority within you, putting to use the awareness that you now have regarding the value and prioritization of your dreams. I want to see you win. In fact, you will win because you now carry a different mentality regarding the success your dreams were meant to achieve. Be careful to not let the negativity of this world suffocate all the great work you've accomplish working through this book. I look forward to benefiting from the value within your dreams.

Become dependent.

Consistently depend on God, for this is what fuels the strength and courage you will need to carry out the purpose your life was meant for. Our greatest reward is that we don't have to figure out this thing called life all on our own. Be careful to maintain your dependency as a top priority. It is our ear in tune to the mouth of God that leads to discovering the eternal value in our lives. Dependency is where we attain our reassurance, where God reminds us to be fearless and to not be afraid or discouraged by whatever circumstances we face. It's the place where a steady dialogue with the Father tunes our ear to what's on His heart, so that we may be prosperous and successful. This gives us the confidence knowing that the Creator of the universe is on our side and rooting for our success; therefore, He is dependable.

Live with a sense of urgency.

It's been said that we only live once. While this may be true in totality, I would like to enhance this perspective. Think about this: There are twenty-four hours in a day. Out of those twenty-four hours, the average human being spends anywhere between twelve to sixteen hours awake. This equals approximately between 720 to 960 minutes, which equals approximately 57,600 seconds we have at our disposal on a typical day.

Here's the point: You *don't* only live once. You actually have an opportunity to live approximately 12 hours, 960 minutes, or 57,600 seconds each day, so live! Don't undervalue the time you've been given; rather, realize that every day you have an opportunity, a privilege to live. Therefore, maximize every second of it.

> **Here's the point: You don't only live once.**

My final thought is one you've probably heard me say quite often. We all have the opportunity to choose our outlook on life. My hope is that after reading this you will choose from this day on to walk in *The Mentality of Success*—knowing and believing that SUCCESS is truly your destiny!

ACKNOWLEDGMENTS

ACKNOWLEDGMENTS

Too many people have inspired me and contributed to my developing into the man who wrote this book to list them individually. To avoid a Genesis-like genealogy (and in fear of missing someone I cherish), I will instead say: Thank you, all! The value of your lives has added salt and flavor to mine in an incredible way. I am extraordinarily grateful for every single one of you.

To my late grandmother Margaret Lee, thank you for instilling in me at a very young age, seeds of hope and a future that I still benefit from to this day.

To my beautiful wife and son, you are the reason I do any of this. If you weren't in my life, I would be pretty mediocre (It's true!). You inspire me to reach for the stars, so I can give you the world!

To my mother and father Eddie and Rhoderica Washington, thank you for always believing in me and supporting everything I do. Watching the maturation of your lives has inspired me in many ways.

To the guy who has never let a dream die within me . . . Ramces, I love you brother. You are a true rarity in life. I am forever grateful for you. For twenty-two years and counting, we've been inseparable—what a blessing!

To all of you who took the time to read this book, I'd like to thank you. This book carries more than you may ever realize. This framework—*The Mentality Of Success*—not only changed my life, but it saved my life! I share this with you hoping that it will serve you well as you journey through this wonderful challenge called life. Know that I care about your value and your future immensely. Now, go live out the success you were created to live!

ABOUT THE AUTHOR

Having grown up in one of the poorest cities in the United States, Joshua Washington went on to become an organizational psychologist and widely respected expert strategist in personal and professional development. He accomplished this by embracing his own unique ability to translate the complexities of life into a clear roadmap leading to the success he believed he was created and designed to live! He desires nothing more than to do the same for you!

Joshua is a major thought leader, and after nearly a decade of coaching and training senior executive leaders for multimillion-dollar enterprises, he left the corporate world to pursue his passion for serving today's generation by leading it through the process of developing *The Mentality of Success*, so it can recognize it's God-given value and leverage that value in serving others. While originally from Immokalee, Florida, Joshua now lives in Orlando, Florida, with his lovely wife of six years, Valeria Washington, and their lively one-year old son, Nehemiah.

www.ingramcontent.com/pod-product-compliance
Lightning Source LLC
Chambersburg PA
CBHW070541090426
42735CB00013B/3044